ADAM BEECHEN

HENCH

MANNY BELLO

AIT★PLANET LAR
SAN FRANCISCO

HENCH
BY ADAM BEECHEN AND MANNY BELLO

PUBLISHED BY
AIT/PLANET LAR
2034 47TH AVENUE
SAN FRANCISCO, CA 94116

FIRST EDITION: JUNE 2004

10 9 8 7 6 5 4 3 2 1

COVER ILLUSTRATION BY MANNY BELLO
COVER DESIGN BY BRIAN WOOD
BOOK DESIGN BY BRIAN WOOD AND WHISKEY ISLAND
LETTERED BY RYAN (AUXILIARE ET VAPULARE) YOUNT

ISBN: 1-932051-17-1

PRINTED AND BOUND IN CANADA BY QUEBECOR PRINTING, INC.

ADAM BEECHEN

HENCH

MANNY BELLO

ADAM BEECHEN:

FOR STEVE MALAKOWSKY, TEACHER AND FRIEND

MANNY BELLO:

FOR JOSEFINA, JENNIFER AND KATHARINE

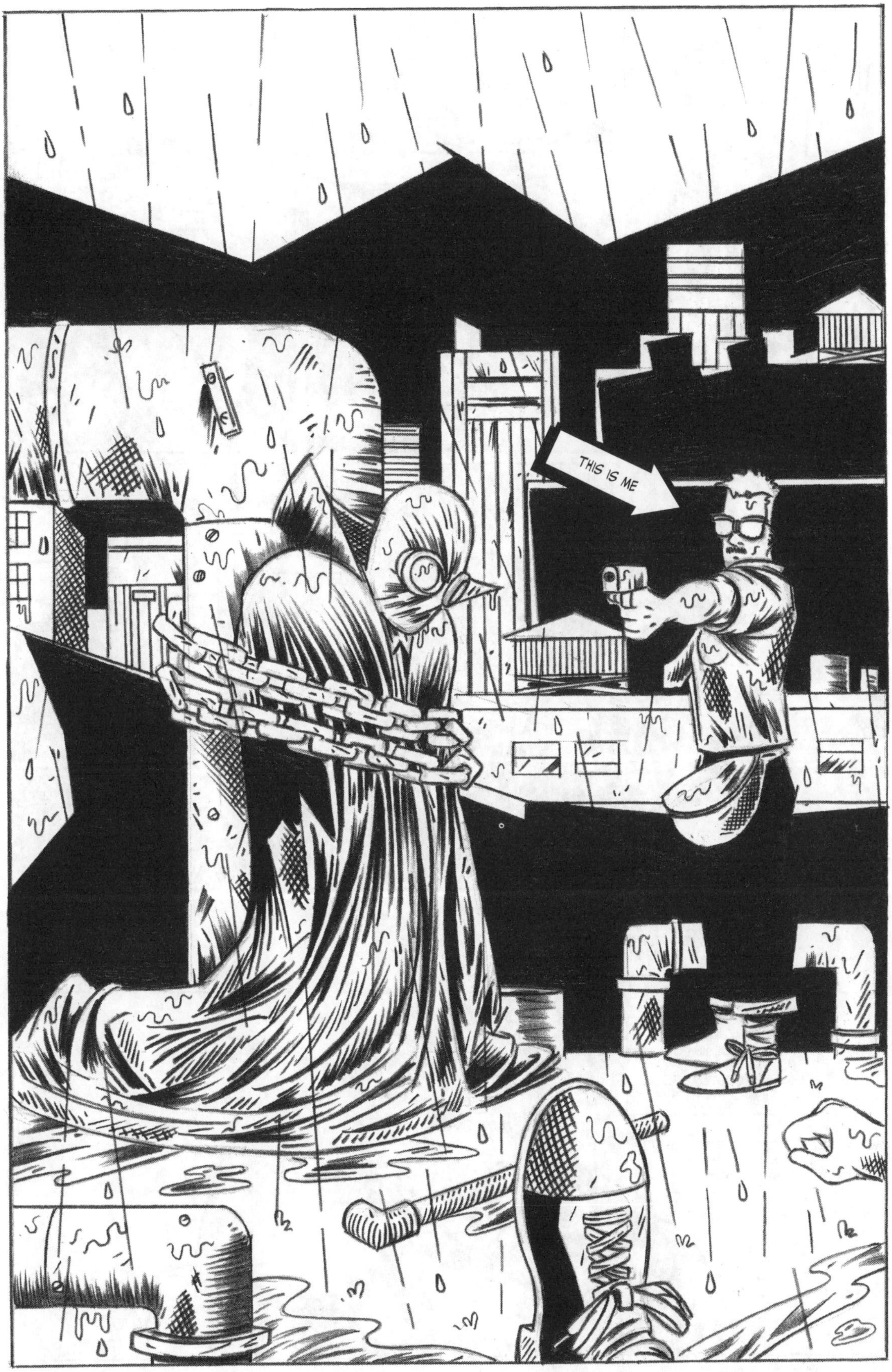
THIS IS ME

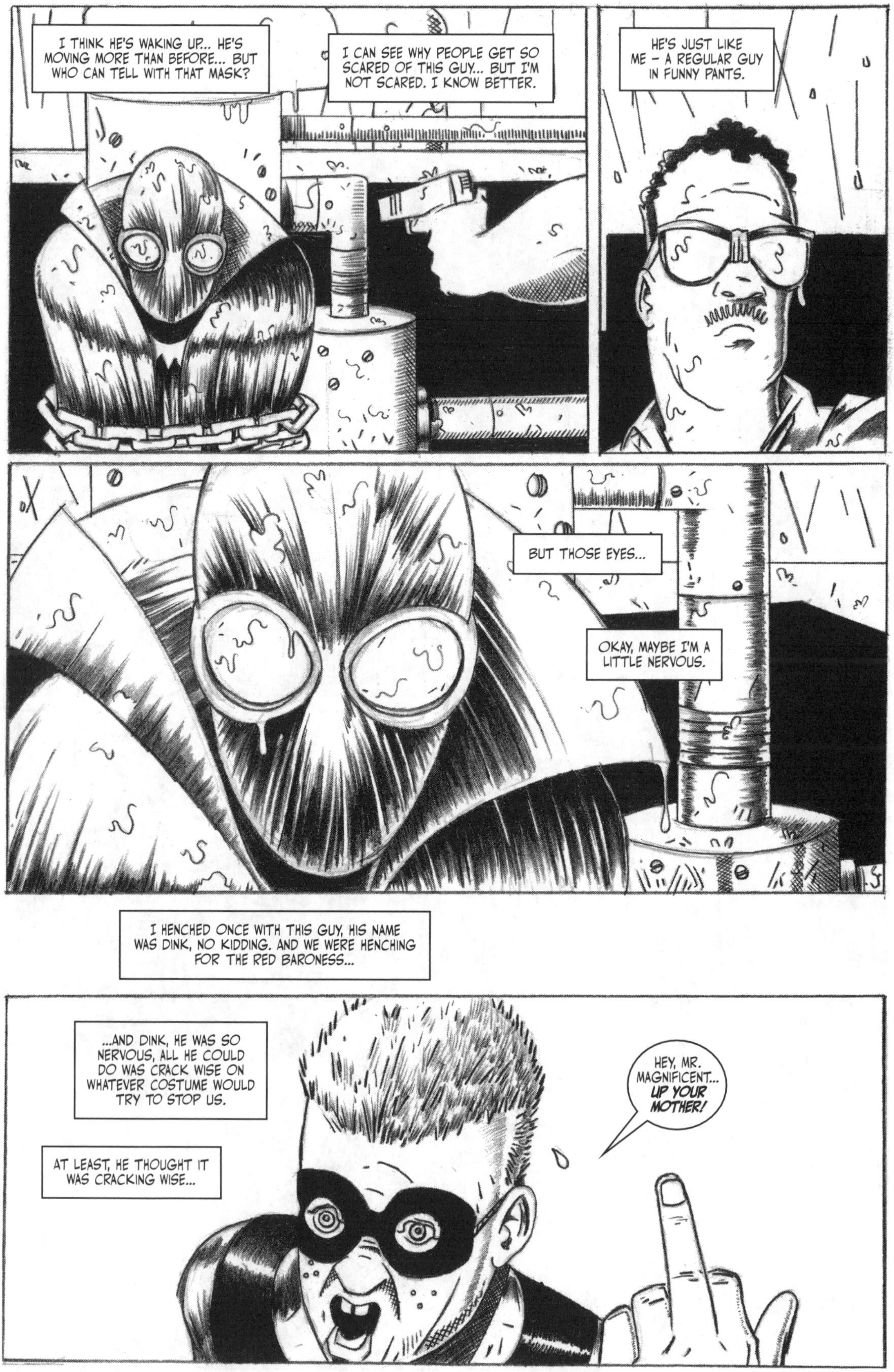
I THINK HE'S WAKING UP... HE'S MOVING MORE THAN BEFORE... BUT WHO CAN TELL WITH THAT MASK?
I CAN SEE WHY PEOPLE GET SO SCARED OF THIS GUY... BUT I'M NOT SCARED. I KNOW BETTER.
HE'S JUST LIKE ME – A REGULAR GUY IN FUNNY PANTS.
BUT THOSE EYES...
OKAY, MAYBE I'M A LITTLE NERVOUS.
I HENCHED ONCE WITH THIS GUY, HIS NAME WAS DINK, NO KIDDING. AND WE WERE HENCHING FOR THE RED BARONESS...
...AND DINK, HE WAS SO NERVOUS, ALL HE COULD DO WAS CRACK WISE ON WHATEVER COSTUME WOULD TRY TO STOP US.
AT LEAST, HE THOUGHT IT WAS CRACKING WISE...
HEY, MR. MAGNIFICENT... ***UP YOUR MOTHER!***

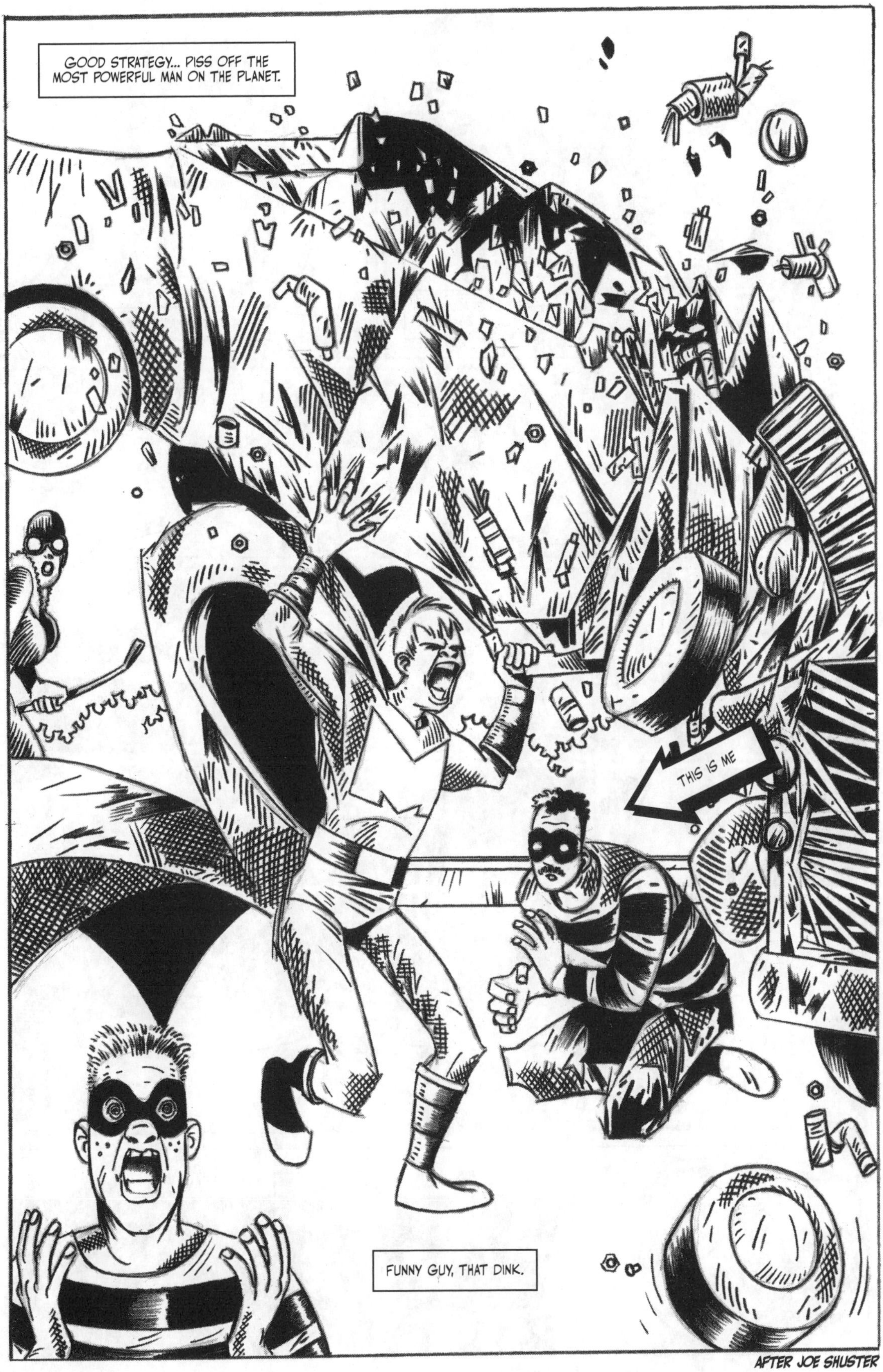
GOOD STRATEGY... PISS OFF THE MOST POWERFUL MAN ON THE PLANET.
THIS IS ME
FUNNY GUY, THAT DINK.

AFTER JOE SHUSTER

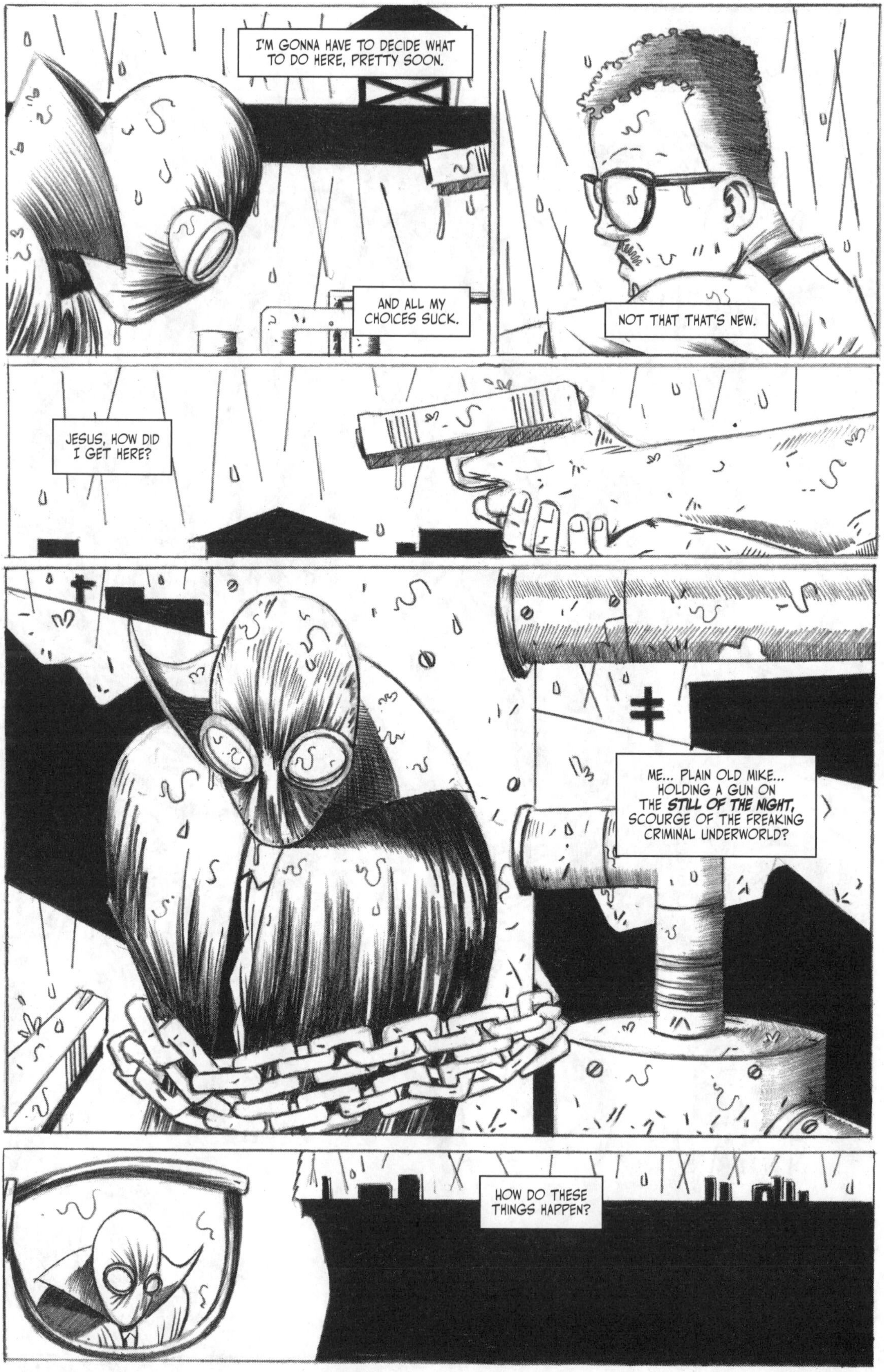

I'M GONNA HAVE TO DECIDE WHAT TO DO HERE, PRETTY SOON.
AND ALL MY CHOICES SUCK.
NOT THAT THAT'S NEW.
JESUS, HOW DID I GET HERE?
ME... PLAIN OLD MIKE... HOLDING A GUN ON THE **STILL OF THE NIGHT,** SCOURGE OF THE FREAKING CRIMINAL UNDERWORLD?
HOW DO THESE THINGS HAPPEN?

I WISH I WAS PLAYING COLLEGE FOOTBALL AGAIN. NOT A DAY GOES BY I HAVEN'T MADE THAT WISH.

ALL THE DECISIONS WERE CLEAR-CUT, BLACK AND WHITE.

GO HERE. HIT THIS GUY. DO IT AGAIN.

HIT SOMEBODY, HIT SOMEBODY, HIT SOMEBODY.

I WAS GOOD AT IT.

I MIGHT HAVE EVEN MADE THE PROS. I HAD WHAT THEY CALL THE "LINEBACKER MENTALITY."

JUST TELL ME WHAT TO DO, AND TURN ME LOOSE.

SORT OF LIKE A GUIDED MISSILE.

I BECAME THE GUY EVERY TEAM BUILT THEIR GAME PLAN ON: TO WIN THE GAME, YOU HAD TO STOP MIKE FULTON.

AND THEN, IN ONE GAME, THE OTHER TEAM TOOK ME OUT.

THEY TOOK ME OUT OF FOOTBALL FOREVER.

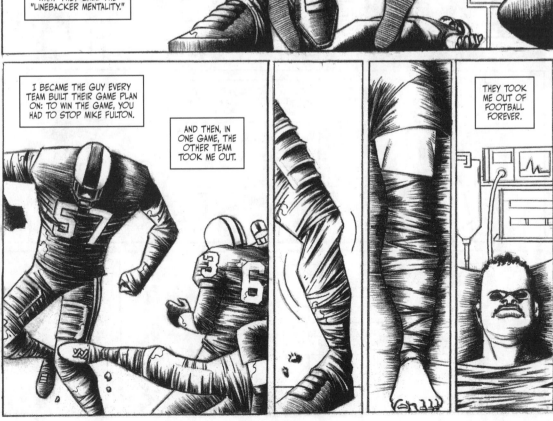

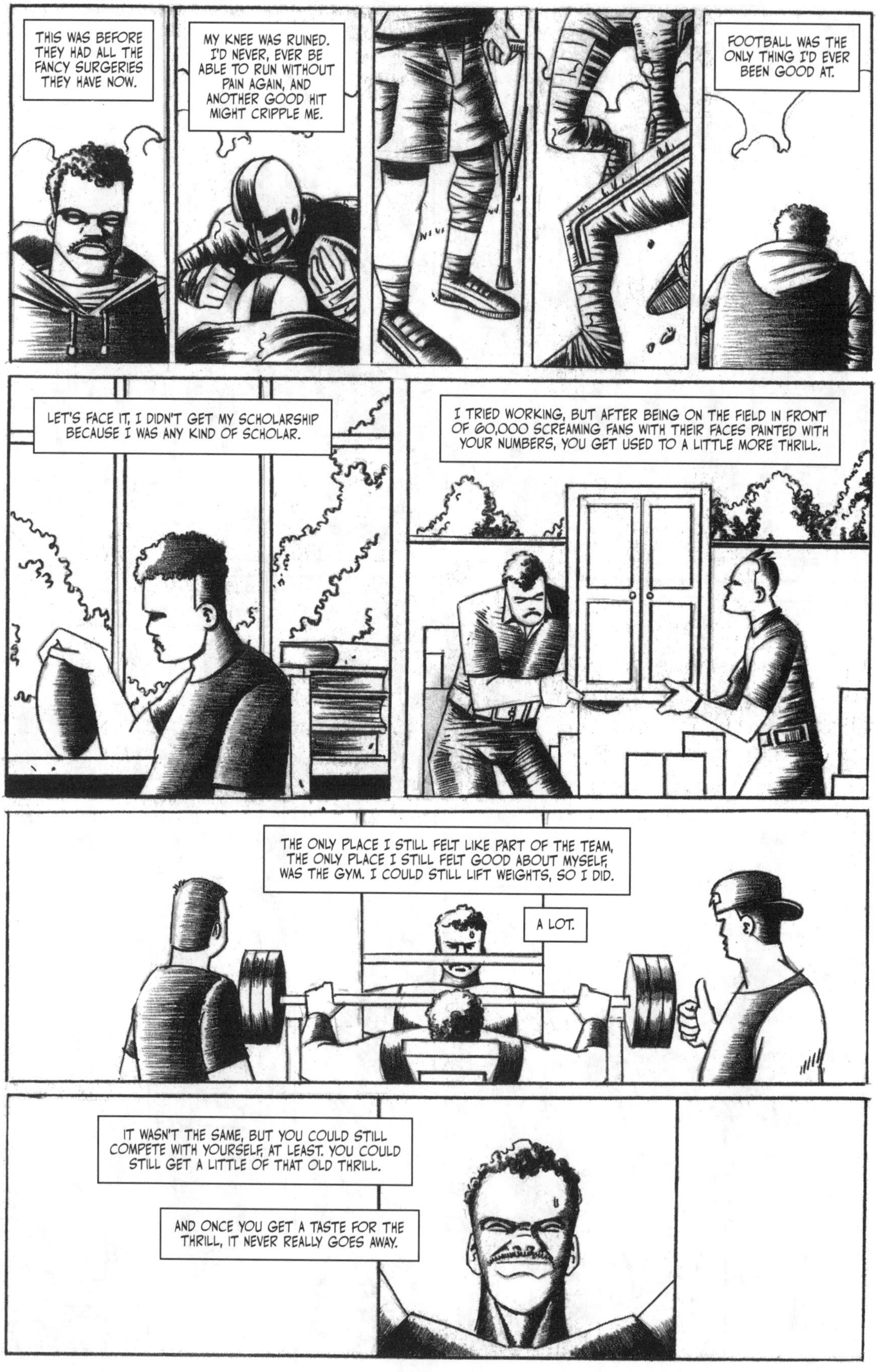
THIS WAS BEFORE THEY HAD ALL THE FANCY SURGERIES THEY HAVE NOW.
MY KNEE WAS RUINED. I'D NEVER, EVER BE ABLE TO RUN WITHOUT PAIN AGAIN, AND ANOTHER GOOD HIT MIGHT CRIPPLE ME.
FOOTBALL WAS THE ONLY THING I'D EVER BEEN GOOD AT.
LET'S FACE IT, I DIDN'T GET MY SCHOLARSHIP BECAUSE I WAS ANY KIND OF SCHOLAR.
I TRIED WORKING, BUT AFTER BEING ON THE FIELD IN FRONT OF 60,000 SCREAMING FANS WITH THEIR FACES PAINTED WITH YOUR NUMBERS, YOU GET USED TO A LITTLE MORE THRILL.
THE ONLY PLACE I STILL FELT LIKE PART OF THE TEAM, THE ONLY PLACE I STILL FELT GOOD ABOUT MYSELF, WAS THE GYM. I COULD STILL LIFT WEIGHTS, SO I DID.
A LOT.
IT WASN'T THE SAME, BUT YOU COULD STILL COMPETE WITH YOURSELF, AT LEAST. YOU COULD STILL GET A LITTLE OF THAT OLD THRILL.
AND ONCE YOU GET A TASTE FOR THE THRILL, IT NEVER REALLY GOES AWAY.

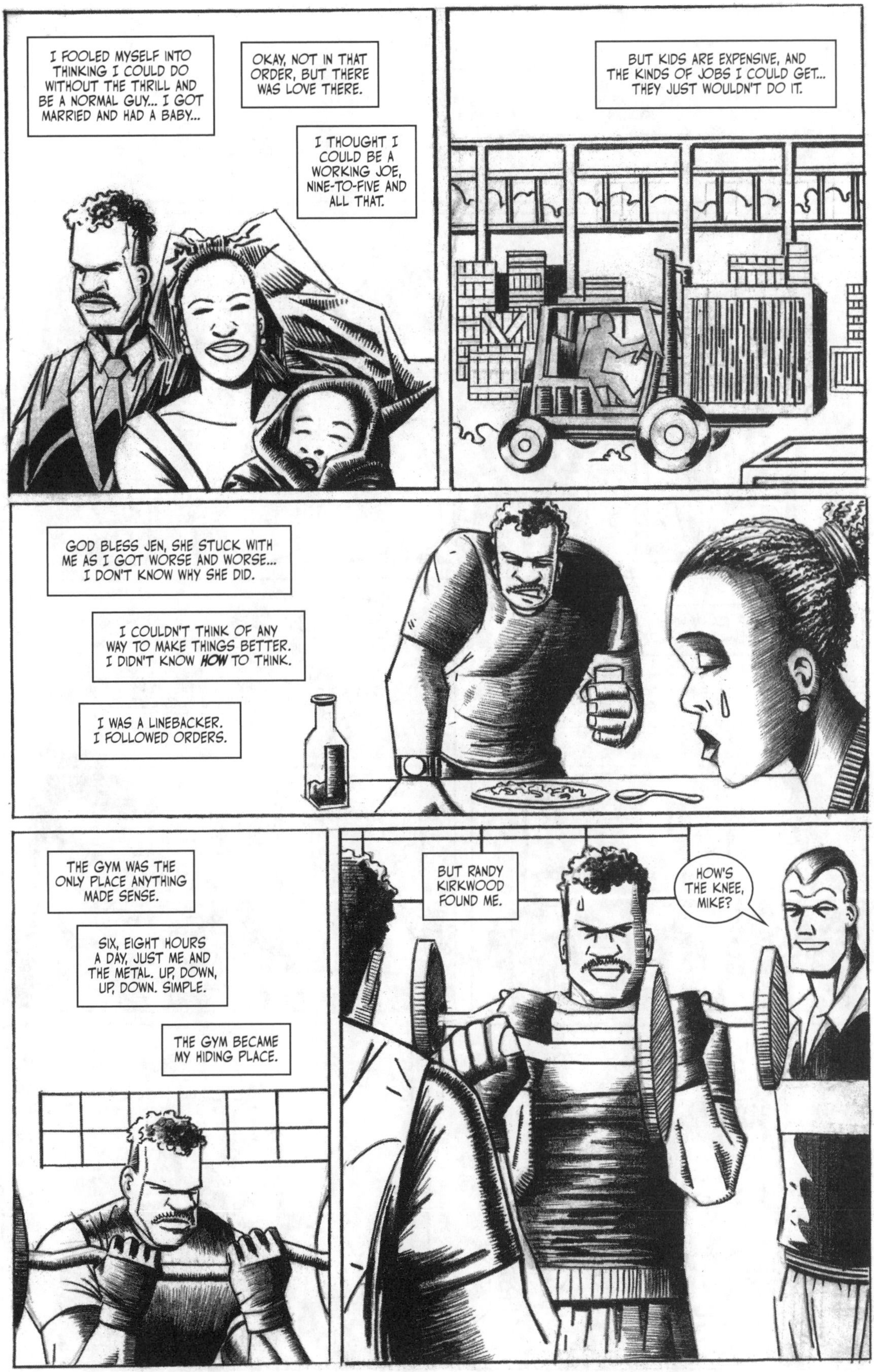
I FOOLED MYSELF INTO THINKING I COULD DO WITHOUT THE THRILL AND BE A NORMAL GUY... I GOT MARRIED AND HAD A BABY...
OKAY, NOT IN THAT ORDER, BUT THERE WAS LOVE THERE.
I THOUGHT I COULD BE A WORKING JOE, NINE-TO-FIVE AND ALL THAT.
BUT KIDS ARE EXPENSIVE, AND THE KINDS OF JOBS I COULD GET... THEY JUST WOULDN'T DO IT.
GOD BLESS JEN, SHE STUCK WITH ME AS I GOT WORSE AND WORSE... I DON'T KNOW WHY SHE DID.
I COULDN'T THINK OF ANY WAY TO MAKE THINGS BETTER. I DIDN'T KNOW *HOW* TO THINK.
I WAS A LINEBACKER. I FOLLOWED ORDERS.
THE GYM WAS THE ONLY PLACE ANYTHING MADE SENSE.
SIX, EIGHT HOURS A DAY, JUST ME AND THE METAL. UP, DOWN, UP, DOWN. SIMPLE.
THE GYM BECAME MY HIDING PLACE.
BUT RANDY KIRKWOOD FOUND ME.
HOW'S THE KNEE, MIKE?

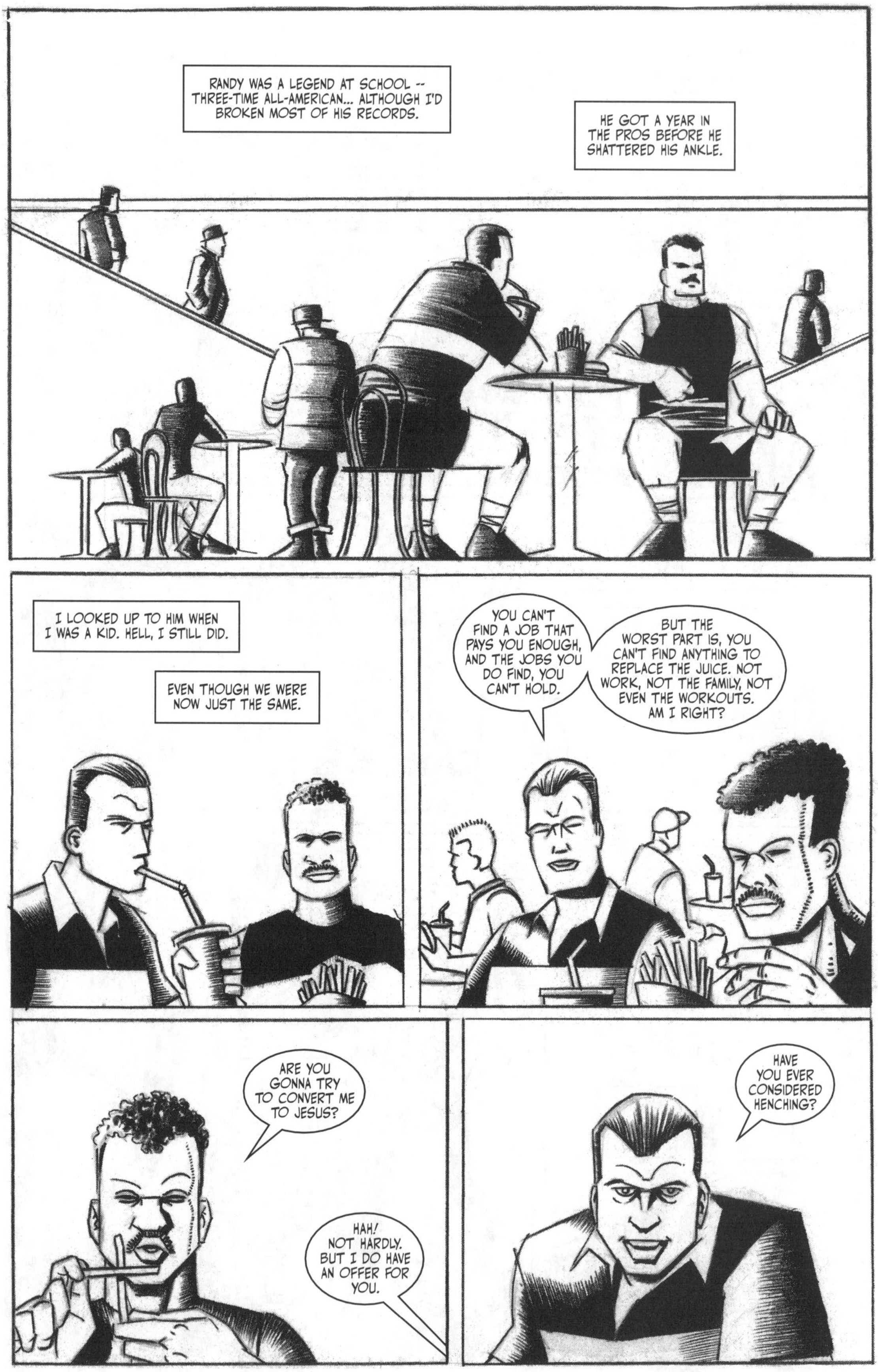
RANDY WAS A LEGEND AT SCHOOL -- THREE-TIME ALL-AMERICAN... ALTHOUGH I'D BROKEN MOST OF HIS RECORDS.
HE GOT A YEAR IN THE PROS BEFORE HE SHATTERED HIS ANKLE.
I LOOKED UP TO HIM WHEN I WAS A KID. HELL, I STILL DID.
EVEN THOUGH WE WERE NOW JUST THE SAME.
YOU CAN'T FIND A JOB THAT PAYS YOU ENOUGH, AND THE JOBS YOU DO FIND, YOU CAN'T HOLD.
BUT THE WORST PART IS, YOU CAN'T FIND ANYTHING TO REPLACE THE JUICE. NOT WORK, NOT THE FAMILY, NOT EVEN THE WORKOUTS. AM I RIGHT?
ARE YOU GONNA TRY TO CONVERT ME TO JESUS?
HAH! NOT HARDLY. BUT I DO HAVE AN OFFER FOR YOU.
HAVE YOU EVER CONSIDERED HENCHING?

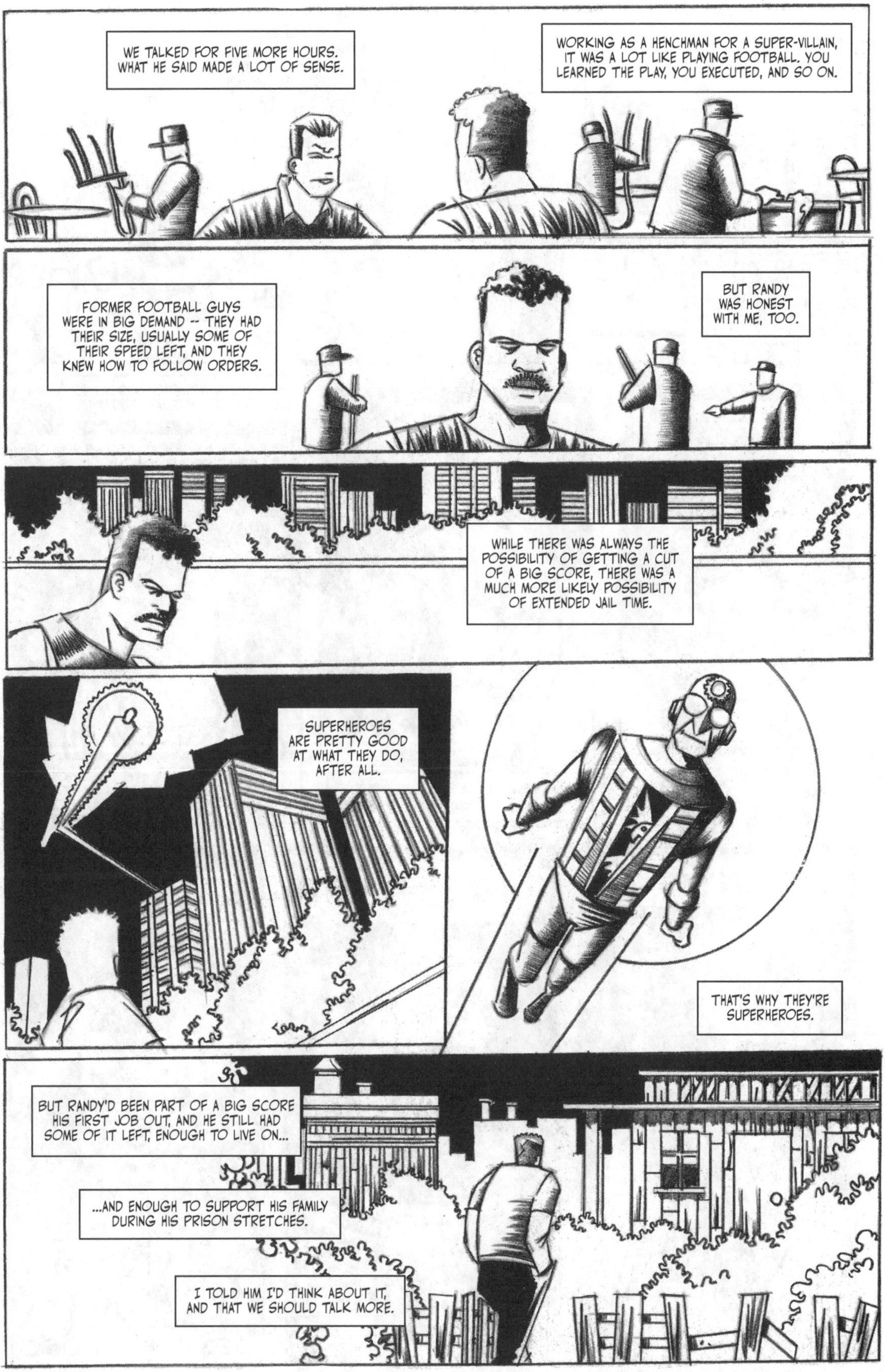

WE TALKED FOR FIVE MORE HOURS. WHAT HE SAID MADE A LOT OF SENSE.
WORKING AS A HENCHMAN FOR A SUPER-VILLAIN, IT WAS A LOT LIKE PLAYING FOOTBALL. YOU LEARNED THE PLAY, YOU EXECUTED, AND SO ON.
FORMER FOOTBALL GUYS WERE IN BIG DEMAND -- THEY HAD THEIR SIZE, USUALLY SOME OF THEIR SPEED LEFT, AND THEY KNEW HOW TO FOLLOW ORDERS.
BUT RANDY WAS HONEST WITH ME, TOO.
WHILE THERE WAS ALWAYS THE POSSIBILITY OF GETTING A CUT OF A BIG SCORE, THERE WAS A MUCH MORE LIKELY POSSIBILITY OF EXTENDED JAIL TIME.
SUPERHEROES ARE PRETTY GOOD AT WHAT THEY DO, AFTER ALL.
THAT'S WHY THEY'RE SUPERHEROES.
BUT RANDY'D BEEN PART OF A BIG SCORE HIS FIRST JOB OUT, AND HE STILL HAD SOME OF IT LEFT, ENOUGH TO LIVE ON...
...AND ENOUGH TO SUPPORT HIS FAMILY DURING HIS PRISON STRETCHES.
I TOLD HIM I'D THINK ABOUT IT, AND THAT WE SHOULD TALK MORE.

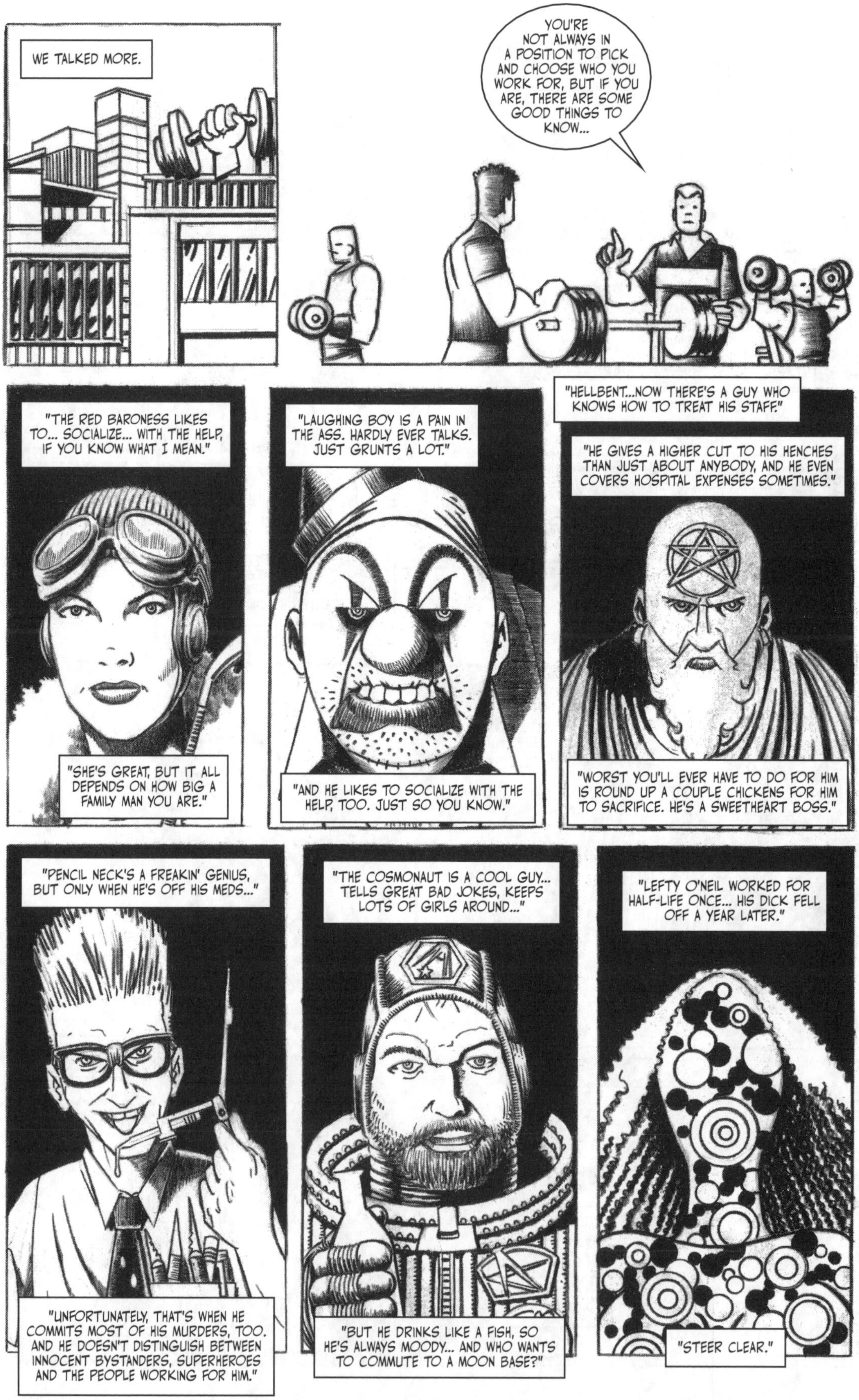
WE TALKED MORE.
YOU'RE NOT ALWAYS IN A POSITION TO PICK AND CHOOSE WHO YOU WORK FOR, BUT IF YOU ARE, THERE ARE SOME GOOD THINGS TO KNOW...
"THE RED BARONESS LIKES TO... SOCIALIZE... WITH THE HELP, IF YOU KNOW WHAT I MEAN."
"SHE'S GREAT, BUT IT ALL DEPENDS ON HOW BIG A FAMILY MAN YOU ARE."
"LAUGHING BOY IS A PAIN IN THE ASS. HARDLY EVER TALKS. JUST GRUNTS A LOT."
"AND HE LIKES TO SOCIALIZE WITH THE HELP, TOO. JUST SO YOU KNOW."
"HELLBENT...NOW THERE'S A GUY WHO KNOWS HOW TO TREAT HIS STAFF."
"HE GIVES A HIGHER CUT TO HIS HENCHES THAN JUST ABOUT ANYBODY, AND HE EVEN COVERS HOSPITAL EXPENSES SOMETIMES."
"WORST YOU'LL EVER HAVE TO DO FOR HIM IS ROUND UP A COUPLE CHICKENS FOR HIM TO SACRIFICE. HE'S A SWEETHEART BOSS."
"PENCIL NECK'S A FREAKIN' GENIUS, BUT ONLY WHEN HE'S OFF HIS MEDS..."
"UNFORTUNATELY, THAT'S WHEN HE COMMITS MOST OF HIS MURDERS, TOO. AND HE DOESN'T DISTINGUISH BETWEEN INNOCENT BYSTANDERS, SUPERHEROES AND THE PEOPLE WORKING FOR HIM."
"THE COSMONAUT IS A COOL GUY... TELLS GREAT BAD JOKES, KEEPS LOTS OF GIRLS AROUND..."
"BUT HE DRINKS LIKE A FISH, SO HE'S ALWAYS MOODY... AND WHO WANTS TO COMMUTE TO A MOON BASE?"
"LEFTY O'NEIL WORKED FOR HALF-LIFE ONCE... HIS DICK FELL OFF A YEAR LATER."
"STEER CLEAR."

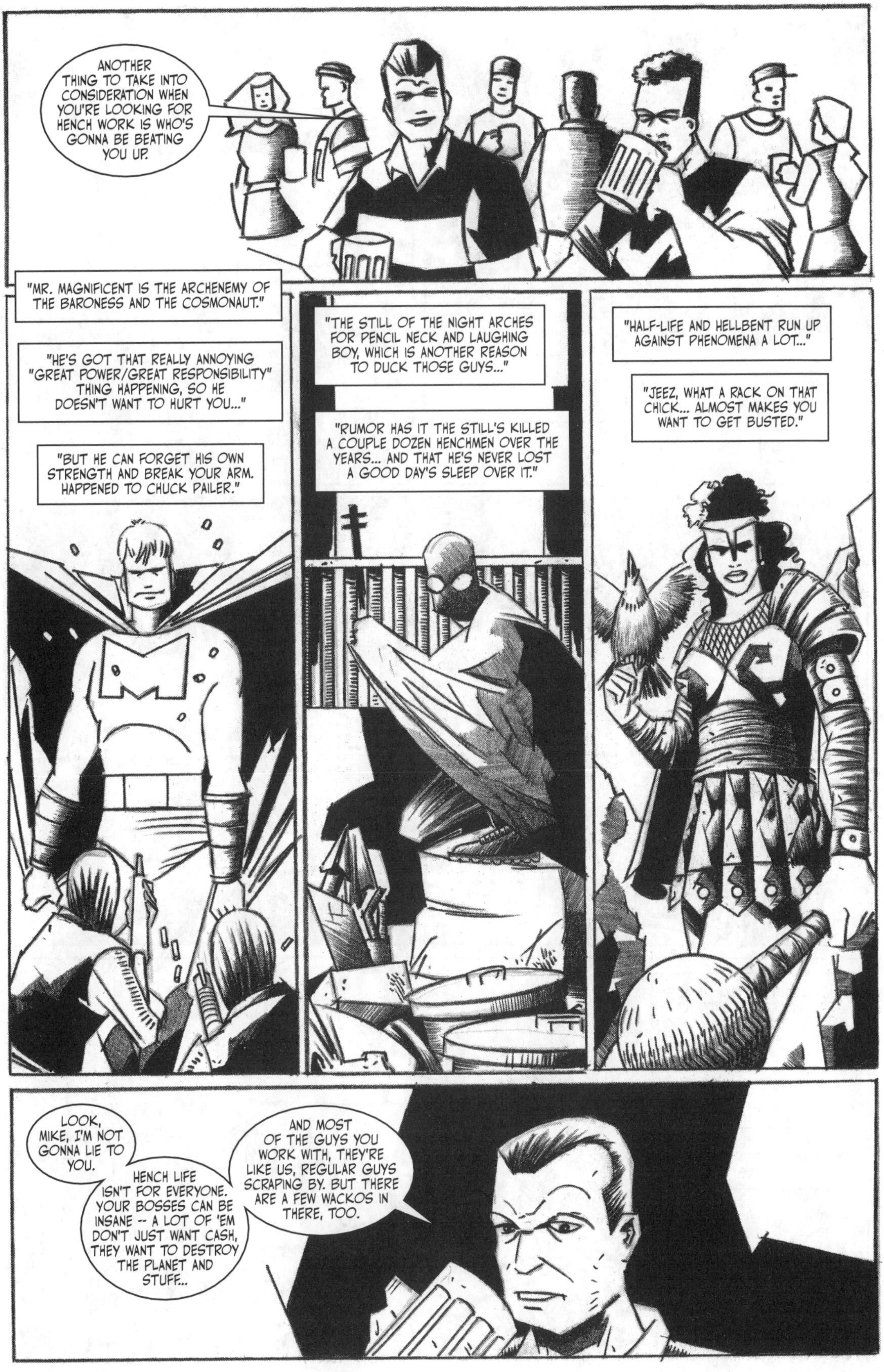
ANOTHER THING TO TAKE INTO CONSIDERATION WHEN YOU'RE LOOKING FOR HENCH WORK IS WHO'S GONNA BE BEATING YOU UP.
"MR. MAGNIFICENT IS THE ARCHENEMY OF THE BARONESS AND THE COSMONAUT."
"HE'S GOT THAT REALLY ANNOYING "GREAT POWER/GREAT RESPONSIBILITY" THING HAPPENING, SO HE DOESN'T WANT TO HURT YOU..."
"BUT HE CAN FORGET HIS OWN STRENGTH AND BREAK YOUR ARM. HAPPENED TO CHUCK PAILER."
"THE STILL OF THE NIGHT ARCHES FOR PENCIL NECK AND LAUGHING BOY, WHICH IS ANOTHER REASON TO DUCK THOSE GUYS..."
"RUMOR HAS IT THE STILL'S KILLED A COUPLE DOZEN HENCHMEN OVER THE YEARS... AND THAT HE'S NEVER LOST A GOOD DAY'S SLEEP OVER IT."
"HALF-LIFE AND HELLBENT RUN UP AGAINST PHENOMENA A LOT..."
"JEEZ, WHAT A RACK ON THAT CHICK... ALMOST MAKES YOU WANT TO GET BUSTED."
LOOK, MIKE, I'M NOT GONNA LIE TO YOU.
HENCH LIFE ISN'T FOR EVERYONE. YOUR BOSSES CAN BE INSANE -- A LOT OF 'EM DON'T JUST WANT CASH, THEY WANT TO DESTROY THE PLANET AND STUFF...
AND MOST OF THE GUYS YOU WORK WITH, THEY'RE LIKE US, REGULAR GUYS SCRAPING BY. BUT THERE ARE A FEW WACKOS IN THERE, TOO.

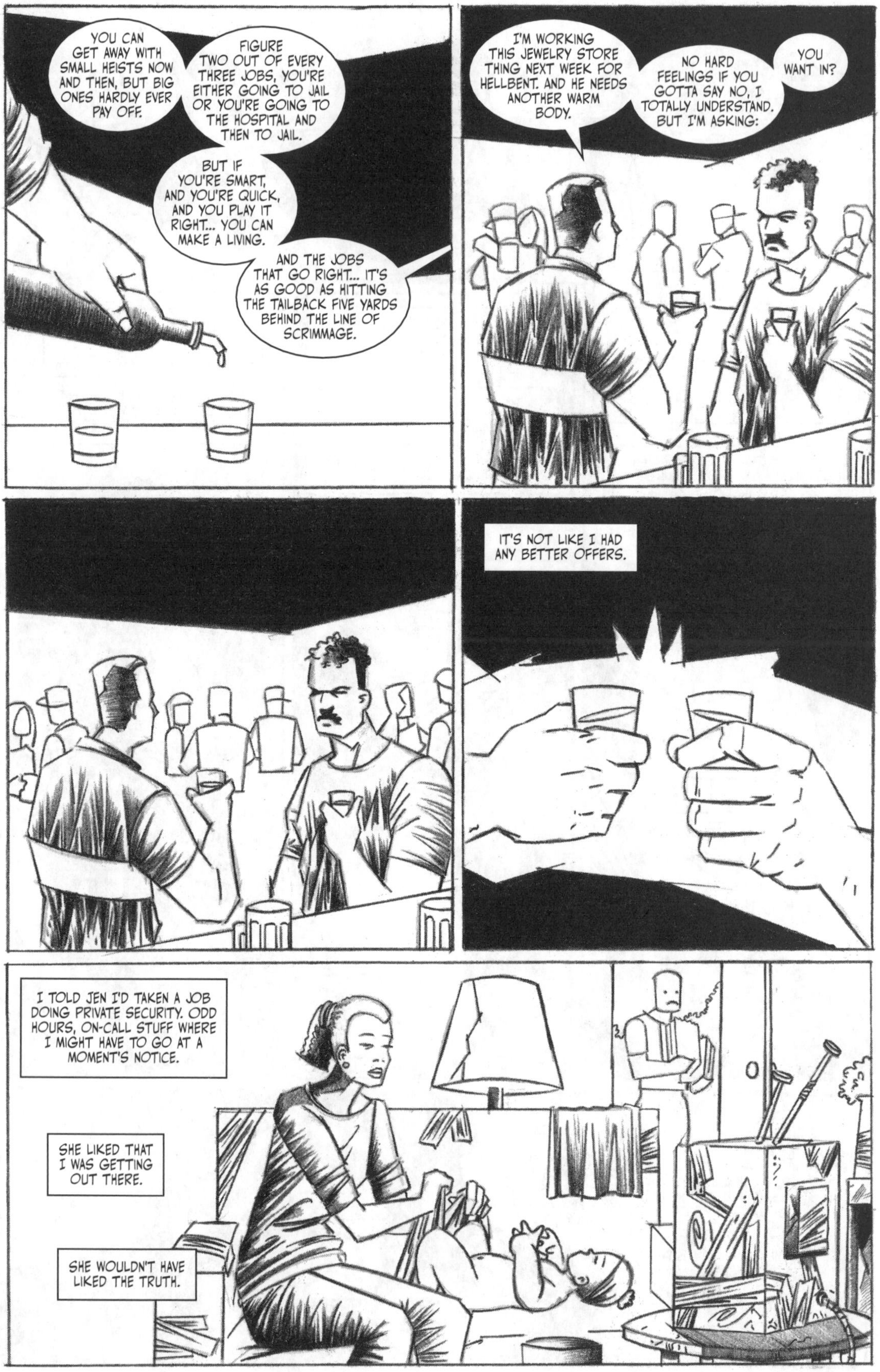
YOU CAN GET AWAY WITH SMALL HEISTS NOW AND THEN, BUT BIG ONES HARDLY EVER PAY OFF.
FIGURE TWO OUT OF EVERY THREE JOBS, YOU'RE EITHER GOING TO JAIL OR YOU'RE GOING TO THE HOSPITAL AND THEN TO JAIL.
BUT IF YOU'RE SMART, AND YOU'RE QUICK, AND YOU PLAY IT RIGHT... YOU CAN MAKE A LIVING.
AND THE JOBS THAT GO RIGHT... IT'S AS GOOD AS HITTING THE TAILBACK FIVE YARDS BEHIND THE LINE OF SCRIMMAGE.
I'M WORKING THIS JEWELRY STORE THING NEXT WEEK FOR HELLBENT. AND HE NEEDS ANOTHER WARM BODY.
NO HARD FEELINGS IF YOU GOTTA SAY NO, I TOTALLY UNDERSTAND. BUT I'M ASKING:
YOU WANT IN?
IT'S NOT LIKE I HAD ANY BETTER OFFERS.
I TOLD JEN I'D TAKEN A JOB DOING PRIVATE SECURITY. ODD HOURS, ON-CALL STUFF WHERE I MIGHT HAVE TO GO AT A MOMENT'S NOTICE.
SHE LIKED THAT I WAS GETTING OUT THERE.
SHE WOULDN'T HAVE LIKED THE TRUTH.

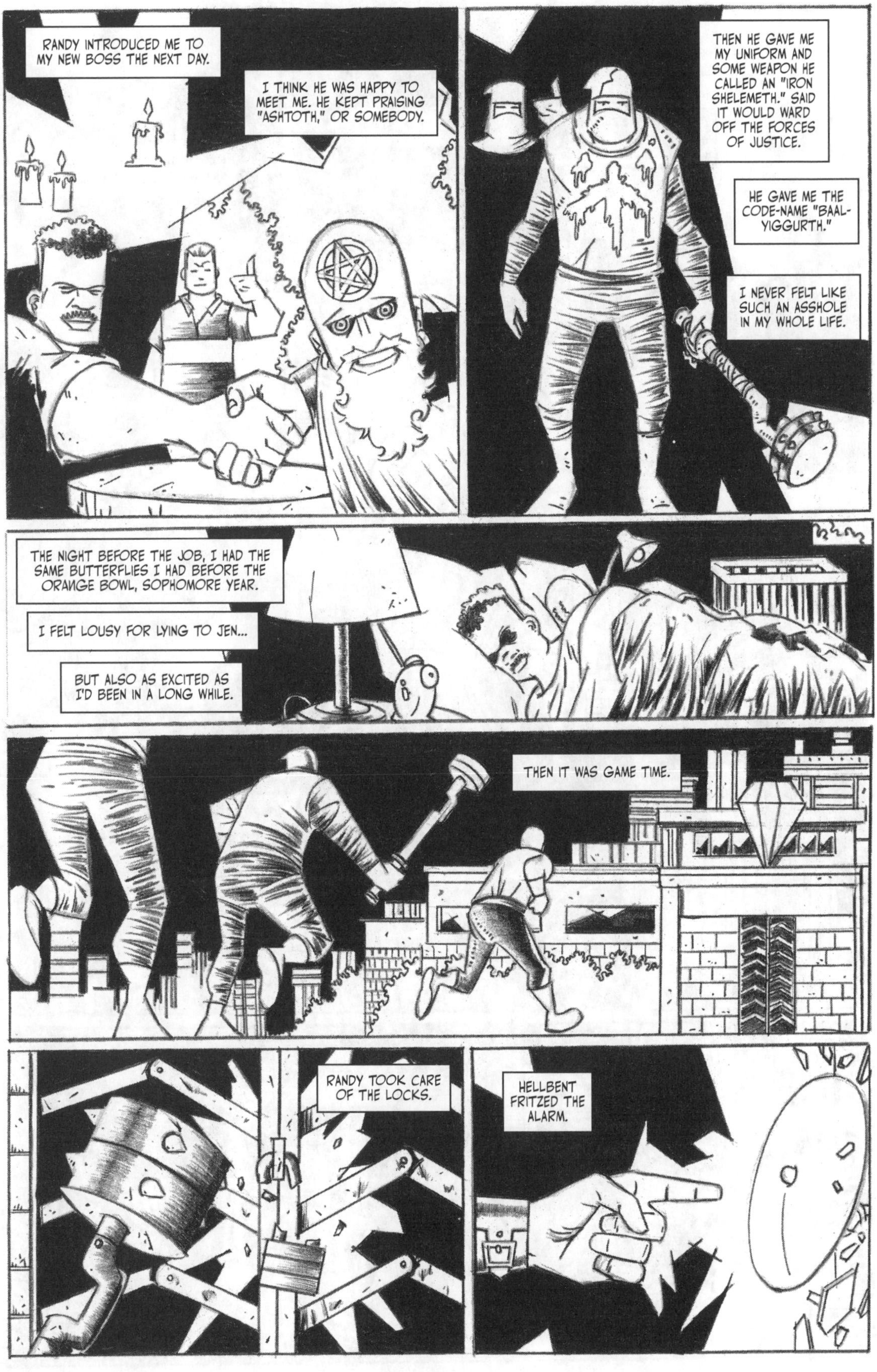
RANDY INTRODUCED ME TO MY NEW BOSS THE NEXT DAY.
I THINK HE WAS HAPPY TO MEET ME. HE KEPT PRAISING "ASHTOTH," OR SOMEBODY.
THEN HE GAVE ME MY UNIFORM AND SOME WEAPON HE CALLED AN "IRON SHELEMETH." SAID IT WOULD WARD OFF THE FORCES OF JUSTICE.
HE GAVE ME THE CODE-NAME "BAAL-YIGGURTH."
I NEVER FELT LIKE SUCH AN ASSHOLE IN MY WHOLE LIFE.
THE NIGHT BEFORE THE JOB, I HAD THE SAME BUTTERFLIES I HAD BEFORE THE ORANGE BOWL, SOPHOMORE YEAR.
I FELT LOUSY FOR LYING TO JEN...
BUT ALSO AS EXCITED AS I'D BEEN IN A LONG WHILE.
THEN IT WAS GAME TIME.
RANDY TOOK CARE OF THE LOCKS.
HELLBENT FRITZED THE ALARM.

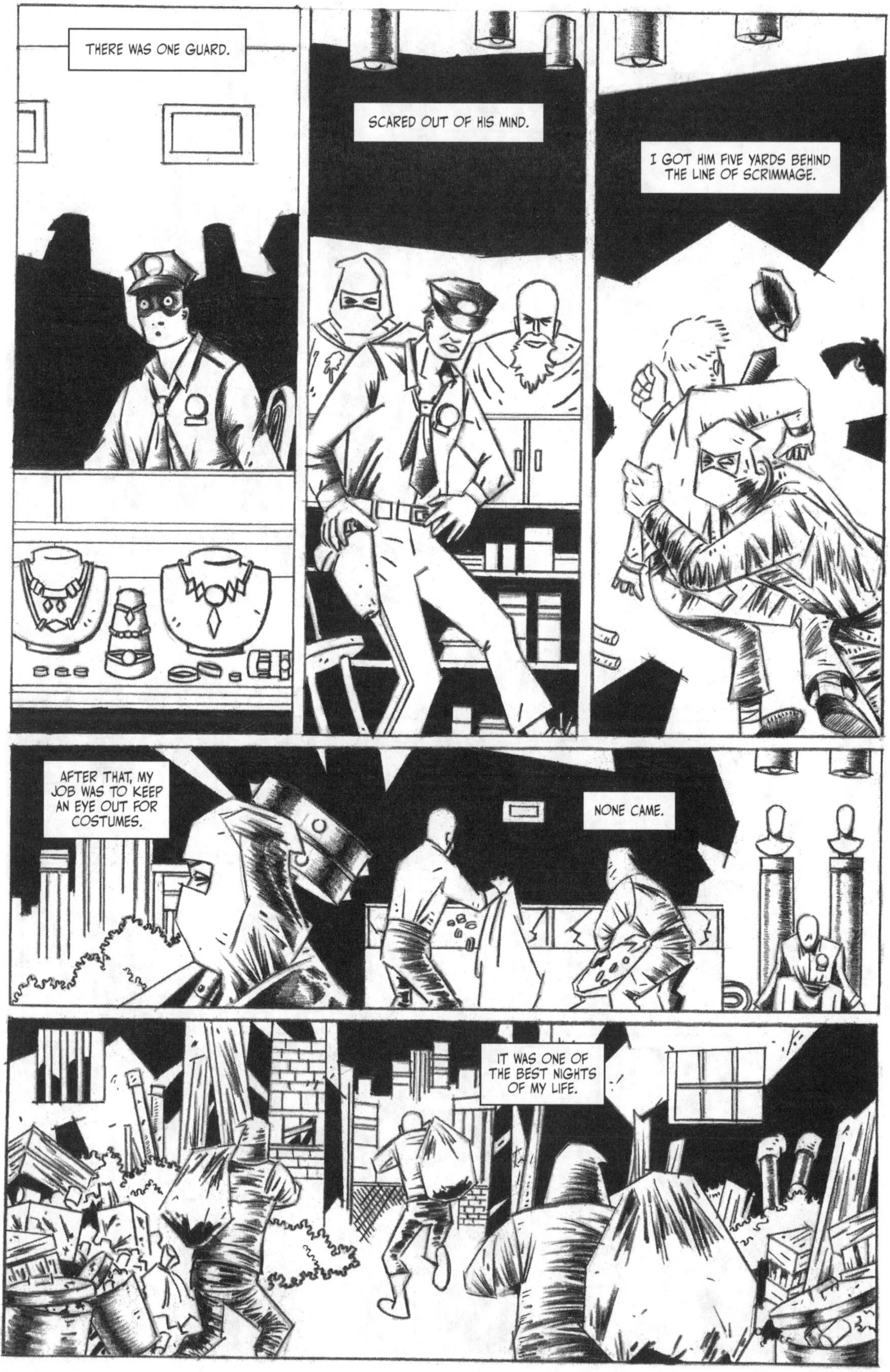
THERE WAS ONE GUARD.
SCARED OUT OF HIS MIND.
I GOT HIM FIVE YARDS BEHIND THE LINE OF SCRIMMAGE.
AFTER THAT, MY JOB WAS TO KEEP AN EYE OUT FOR COSTUMES.
NONE CAME.
IT WAS ONE OF THE BEST NIGHTS OF MY LIFE.

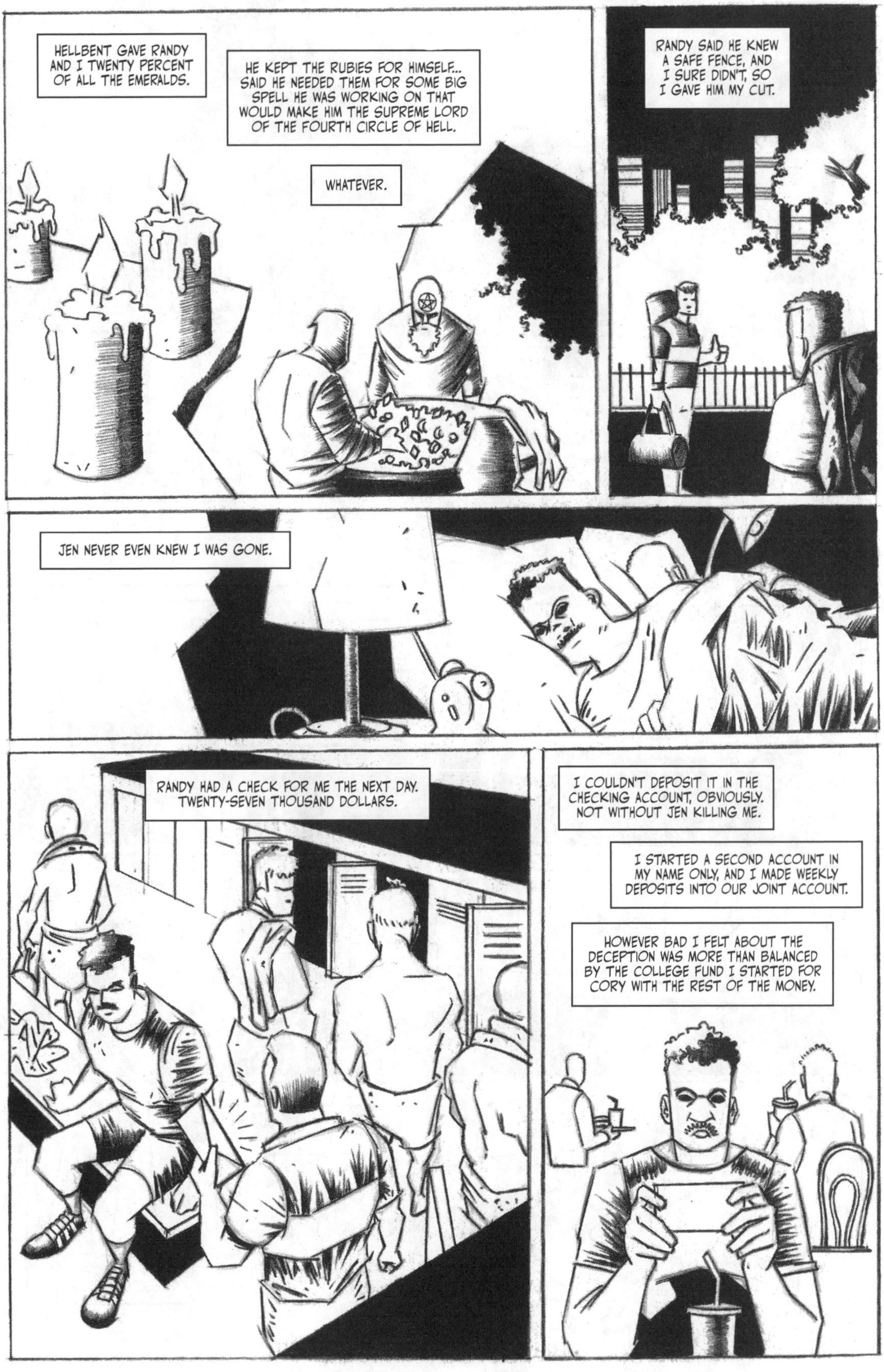
HELLBENT GAVE RANDY AND I TWENTY PERCENT OF ALL THE EMERALDS.
HE KEPT THE RUBIES FOR HIMSELF... SAID HE NEEDED THEM FOR SOME BIG SPELL HE WAS WORKING ON THAT WOULD MAKE HIM THE SUPREME LORD OF THE FOURTH CIRCLE OF HELL.
WHATEVER.
RANDY SAID HE KNEW A SAFE FENCE, AND I SURE DIDN'T, SO I GAVE HIM MY CUT.
JEN NEVER EVEN KNEW I WAS GONE.
RANDY HAD A CHECK FOR ME THE NEXT DAY. TWENTY-SEVEN THOUSAND DOLLARS.
I COULDN'T DEPOSIT IT IN THE CHECKING ACCOUNT, OBVIOUSLY. NOT WITHOUT JEN KILLING ME.
I STARTED A SECOND ACCOUNT IN MY NAME ONLY, AND I MADE WEEKLY DEPOSITS INTO OUR JOINT ACCOUNT.
HOWEVER BAD I FELT ABOUT THE DECEPTION WAS MORE THAN BALANCED BY THE COLLEGE FUND I STARTED FOR CORY WITH THE REST OF THE MONEY.

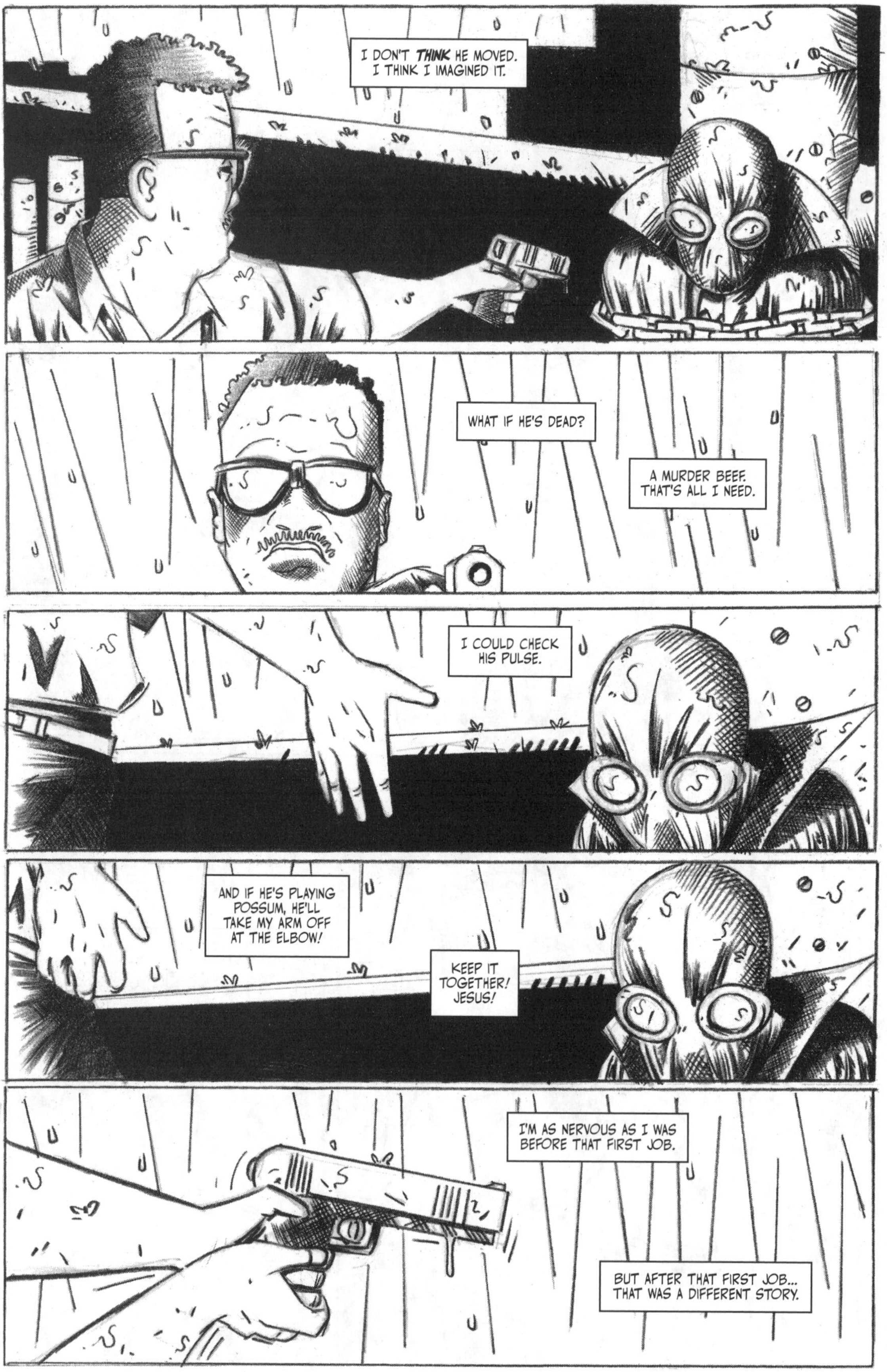

I DON'T THINK HE MOVED. I THINK I IMAGINED IT.
WHAT IF HE'S DEAD?
A MURDER BEEF. THAT'S ALL I NEED.
I COULD CHECK HIS PULSE.
AND IF HE'S PLAYING POSSUM, HE'LL TAKE MY ARM OFF AT THE ELBOW!
KEEP IT TOGETHER! JESUS!
I'M AS NERVOUS AS I WAS BEFORE THAT FIRST JOB.
BUT AFTER THAT FIRST JOB... THAT WAS A DIFFERENT STORY.

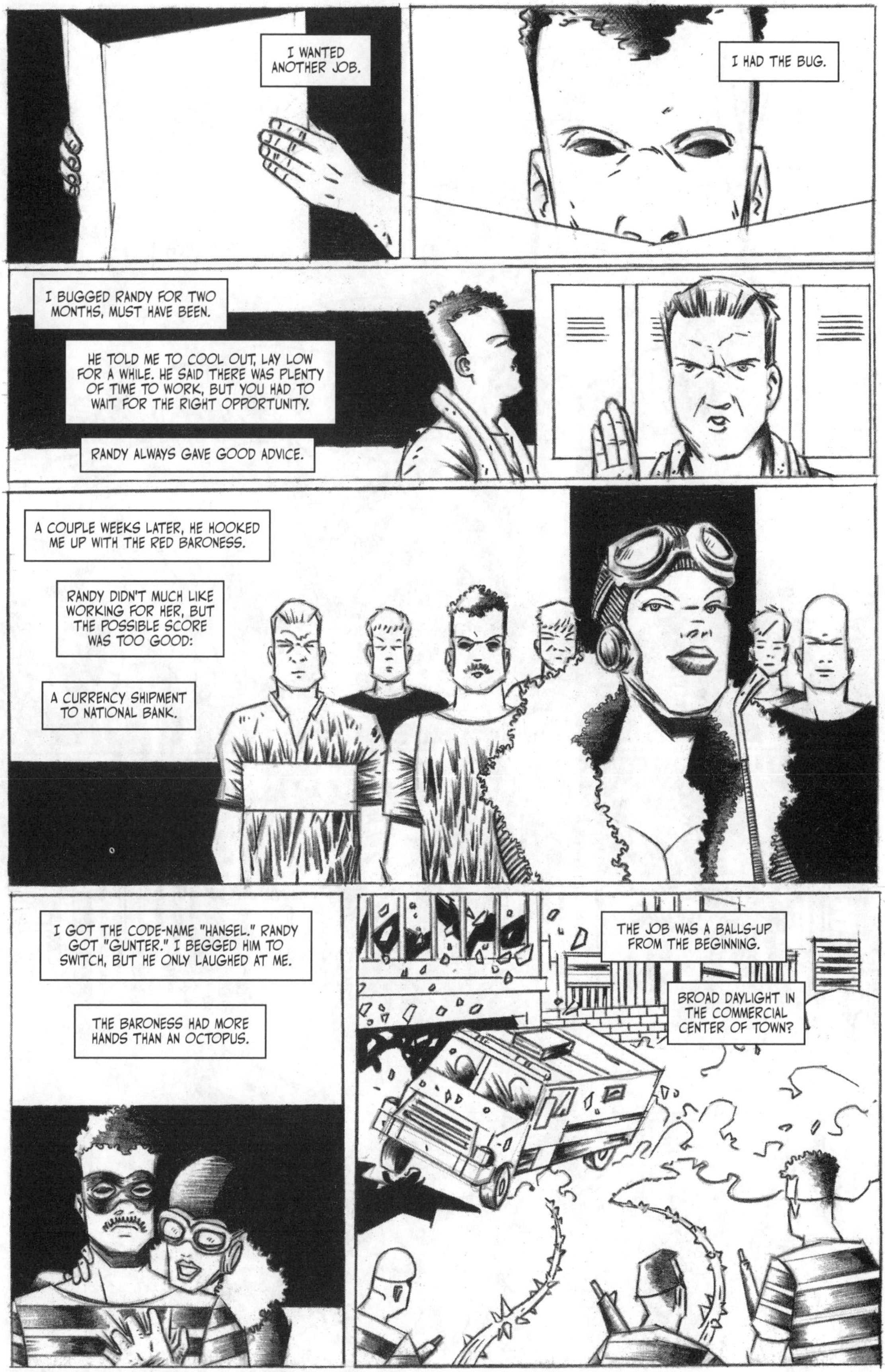
I WANTED ANOTHER JOB.
I HAD THE BUG.
I BUGGED RANDY FOR TWO MONTHS, MUST HAVE BEEN.
HE TOLD ME TO COOL OUT, LAY LOW FOR A WHILE. HE SAID THERE WAS PLENTY OF TIME TO WORK, BUT YOU HAD TO WAIT FOR THE RIGHT OPPORTUNITY.
RANDY ALWAYS GAVE GOOD ADVICE.
A COUPLE WEEKS LATER, HE HOOKED ME UP WITH THE RED BARONESS.
RANDY DIDN'T MUCH LIKE WORKING FOR HER, BUT THE POSSIBLE SCORE WAS TOO GOOD:
A CURRENCY SHIPMENT TO NATIONAL BANK.
I GOT THE CODE-NAME "HANSEL." RANDY GOT "GUNTER." I BEGGED HIM TO SWITCH, BUT HE ONLY LAUGHED AT ME.
THE BARONESS HAD MORE HANDS THAN AN OCTOPUS.
THE JOB WAS A BALLS-UP FROM THE BEGINNING.
BROAD DAYLIGHT IN THE COMMERCIAL CENTER OF TOWN?

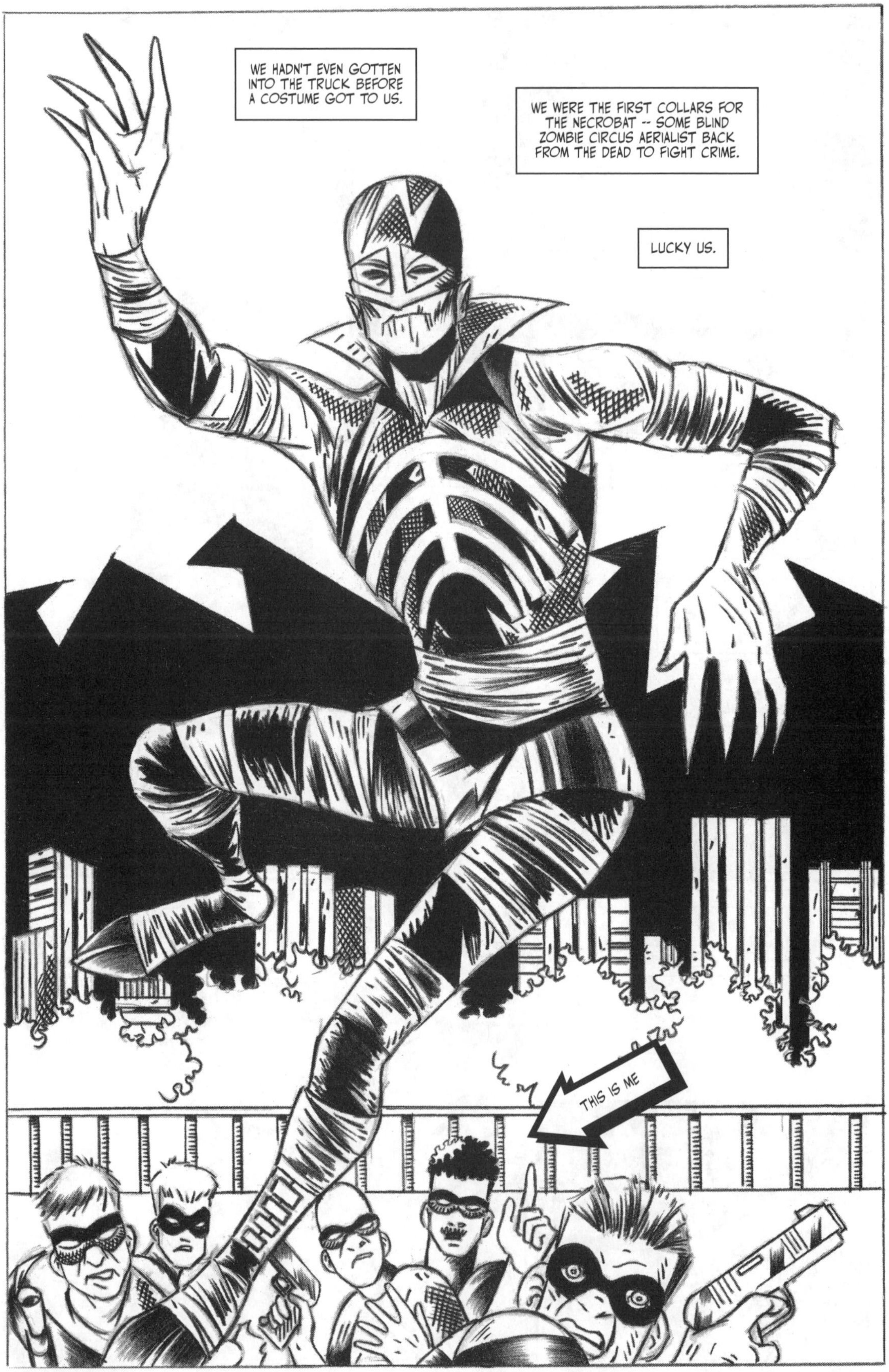
WE HADN'T EVEN GOTTEN INTO THE TRUCK BEFORE A COSTUME GOT TO US.
WE WERE THE FIRST COLLARS FOR THE NECROBAT -- SOME BLIND ZOMBIE CIRCUS AERIALIST BACK FROM THE DEAD TO FIGHT CRIME.
LUCKY US.
THIS IS ME

AFTER BILL EVERETT

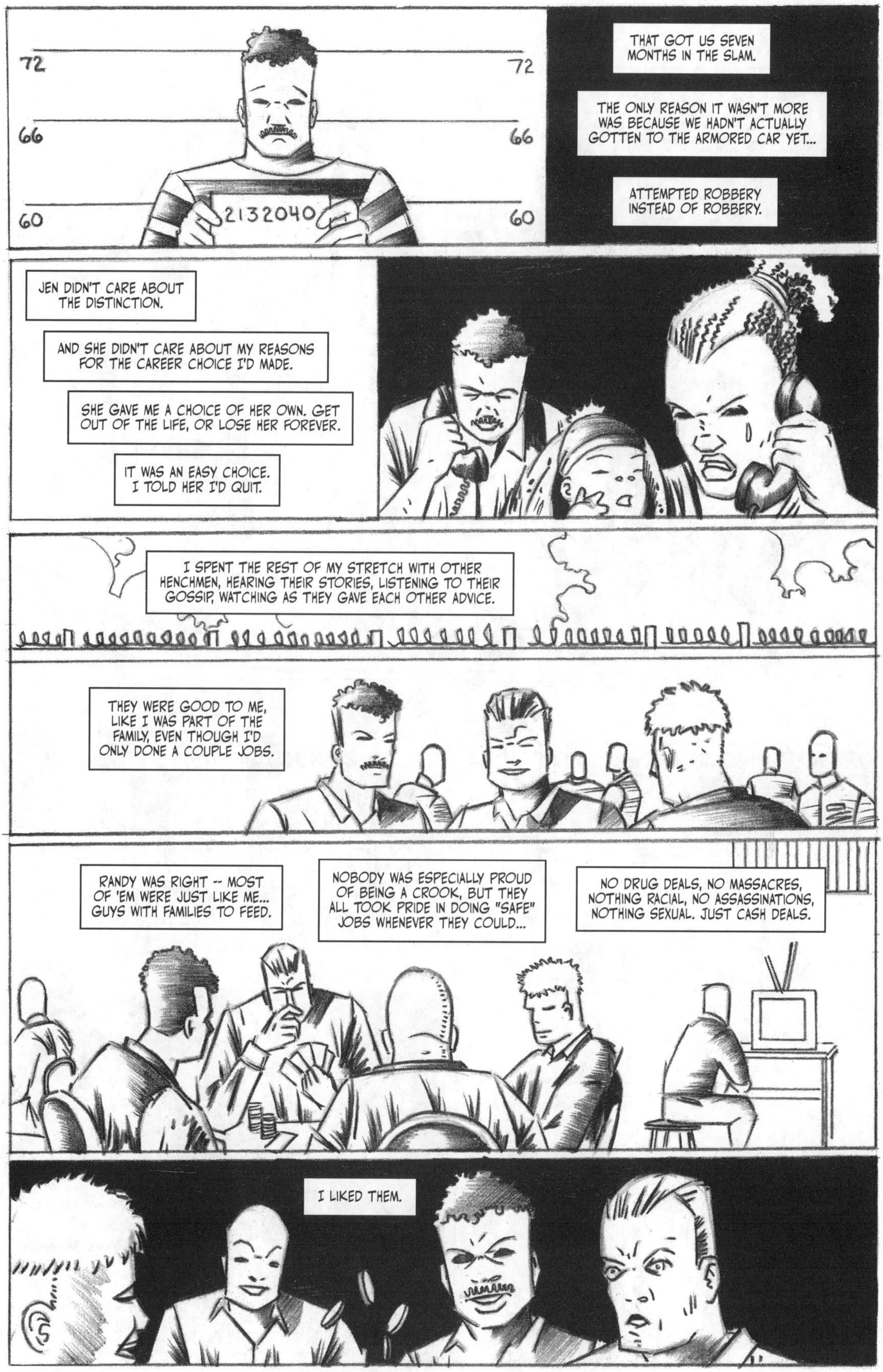
72
72
66
66
60
60
2132040
THAT GOT US SEVEN MONTHS IN THE SLAM.
THE ONLY REASON IT WASN'T MORE WAS BECAUSE WE HADN'T ACTUALLY GOTTEN TO THE ARMORED CAR YET...
ATTEMPTED ROBBERY INSTEAD OF ROBBERY.
JEN DIDN'T CARE ABOUT THE DISTINCTION.
AND SHE DIDN'T CARE ABOUT MY REASONS FOR THE CAREER CHOICE I'D MADE.
SHE GAVE ME A CHOICE OF HER OWN. GET OUT OF THE LIFE, OR LOSE HER FOREVER.
IT WAS AN EASY CHOICE. I TOLD HER I'D QUIT.
I SPENT THE REST OF MY STRETCH WITH OTHER HENCHMEN, HEARING THEIR STORIES, LISTENING TO THEIR GOSSIP, WATCHING AS THEY GAVE EACH OTHER ADVICE.
THEY WERE GOOD TO ME, LIKE I WAS PART OF THE FAMILY, EVEN THOUGH I'D ONLY DONE A COUPLE JOBS.
RANDY WAS RIGHT -- MOST OF 'EM WERE JUST LIKE ME... GUYS WITH FAMILIES TO FEED.
NOBODY WAS ESPECIALLY PROUD OF BEING A CROOK, BUT THEY ALL TOOK PRIDE IN DOING "SAFE" JOBS WHENEVER THEY COULD...
NO DRUG DEALS, NO MASSACRES, NOTHING RACIAL, NO ASSASSINATIONS, NOTHING SEXUAL. JUST CASH DEALS.
I LIKED THEM.

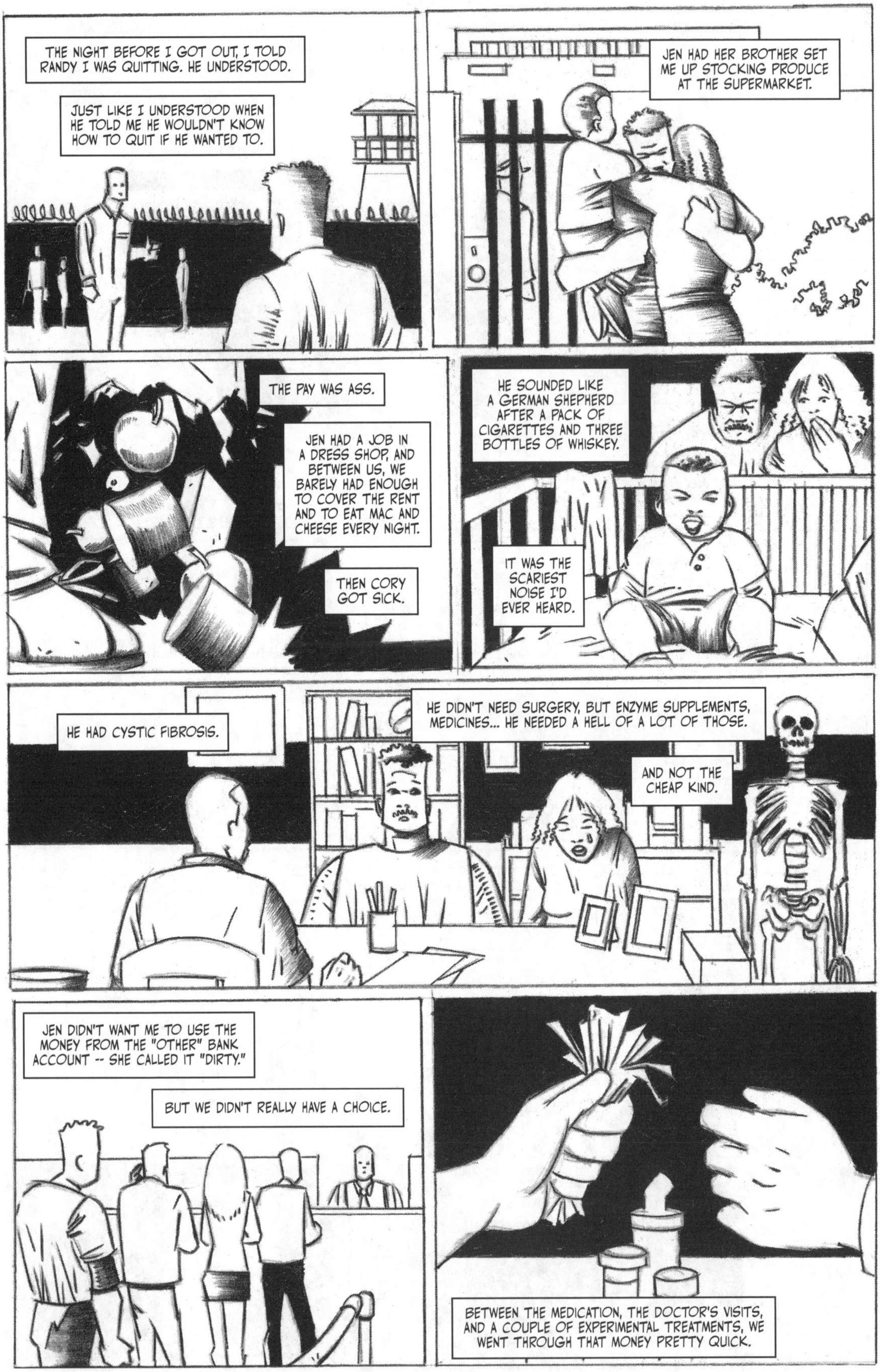
THE NIGHT BEFORE I GOT OUT, I TOLD RANDY I WAS QUITTING. HE UNDERSTOOD.
JUST LIKE I UNDERSTOOD WHEN HE TOLD ME HE WOULDN'T KNOW HOW TO QUIT IF HE WANTED TO.
JEN HAD HER BROTHER SET ME UP STOCKING PRODUCE AT THE SUPERMARKET.
THE PAY WAS ASS.
JEN HAD A JOB IN A DRESS SHOP, AND BETWEEN US, WE BARELY HAD ENOUGH TO COVER THE RENT AND TO EAT MAC AND CHEESE EVERY NIGHT.
THEN CORY GOT SICK.
HE SOUNDED LIKE A GERMAN SHEPHERD AFTER A PACK OF CIGARETTES AND THREE BOTTLES OF WHISKEY.
IT WAS THE SCARIEST NOISE I'D EVER HEARD.
HE HAD CYSTIC FIBROSIS.
HE DIDN'T NEED SURGERY, BUT ENZYME SUPPLEMENTS, MEDICINES... HE NEEDED A HELL OF A LOT OF THOSE.
AND NOT THE CHEAP KIND.
JEN DIDN'T WANT ME TO USE THE MONEY FROM THE "OTHER" BANK ACCOUNT -- SHE CALLED IT "DIRTY."
BUT WE DIDN'T REALLY HAVE A CHOICE.
BETWEEN THE MEDICATION, THE DOCTOR'S VISITS, AND A COUPLE OF EXPERIMENTAL TREATMENTS, WE WENT THROUGH THAT MONEY PRETTY QUICK.

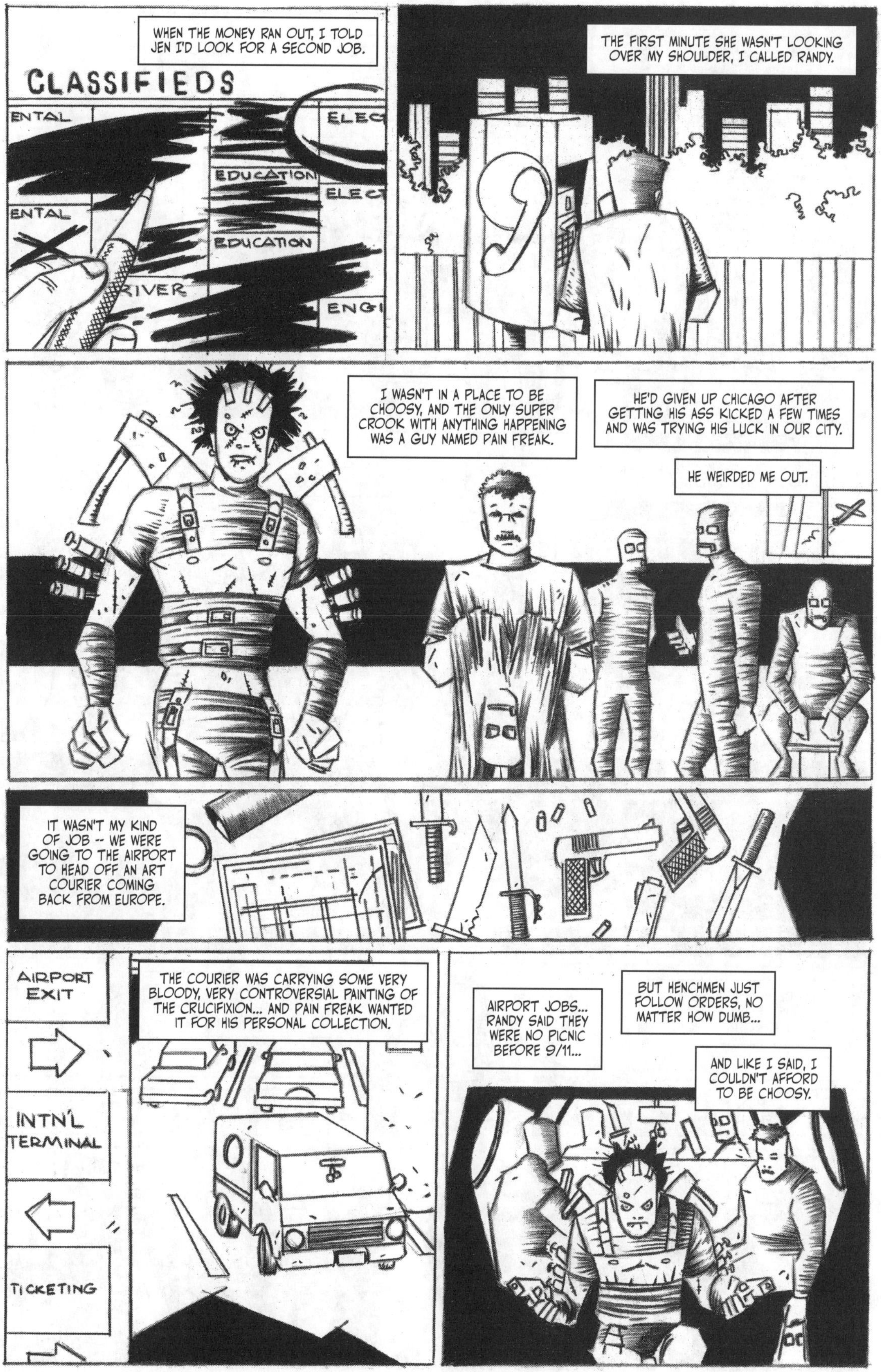
WHEN THE MONEY RAN OUT, I TOLD JEN I'D LOOK FOR A SECOND JOB.
CLASSIFIEDS
ENTAL
ELEC
EDUCATION
ELEC
ENTAL
EDUCATION
RIVER
ENGI
THE FIRST MINUTE SHE WASN'T LOOKING OVER MY SHOULDER, I CALLED RANDY.
I WASN'T IN A PLACE TO BE CHOOSY, AND THE ONLY SUPER CROOK WITH ANYTHING HAPPENING WAS A GUY NAMED PAIN FREAK.
HE'D GIVEN UP CHICAGO AFTER GETTING HIS ASS KICKED A FEW TIMES AND WAS TRYING HIS LUCK IN OUR CITY.
HE WEIRDED ME OUT.
IT WASN'T MY KIND OF JOB -- WE WERE GOING TO THE AIRPORT TO HEAD OFF AN ART COURIER COMING BACK FROM EUROPE.
AIRPORT EXIT
INTN'L TERMINAL
TICKETING
THE COURIER WAS CARRYING SOME VERY BLOODY, VERY CONTROVERSIAL PAINTING OF THE CRUCIFIXION... AND PAIN FREAK WANTED IT FOR HIS PERSONAL COLLECTION.
AIRPORT JOBS... RANDY SAID THEY WERE NO PICNIC BEFORE 9/11...
BUT HENCHMEN JUST FOLLOW ORDERS, NO MATTER HOW DUMB...
AND LIKE I SAID, I COULDN'T AFFORD TO BE CHOOSY.

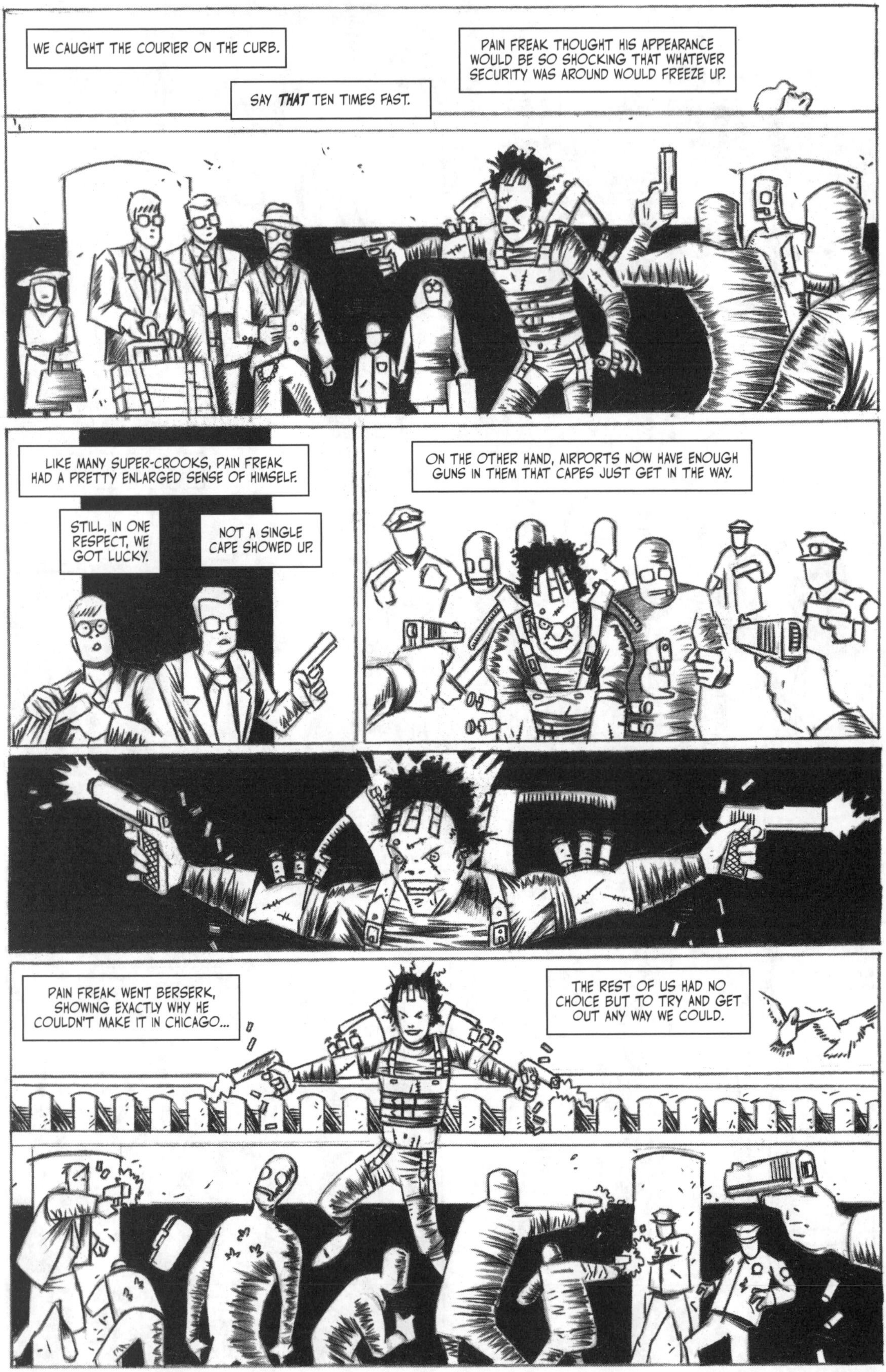
WE CAUGHT THE COURIER ON THE CURB.
SAY THAT TEN TIMES FAST.
PAIN FREAK THOUGHT HIS APPEARANCE WOULD BE SO SHOCKING THAT WHATEVER SECURITY WAS AROUND WOULD FREEZE UP.
LIKE MANY SUPER-CROOKS, PAIN FREAK HAD A PRETTY ENLARGED SENSE OF HIMSELF.
STILL, IN ONE RESPECT, WE GOT LUCKY.
NOT A SINGLE CAPE SHOWED UP.
ON THE OTHER HAND, AIRPORTS NOW HAVE ENOUGH GUNS IN THEM THAT CAPES JUST GET IN THE WAY.
PAIN FREAK WENT BERSERK, SHOWING EXACTLY WHY HE COULDN'T MAKE IT IN CHICAGO...
THE REST OF US HAD NO CHOICE BUT TO TRY AND GET OUT ANY WAY WE COULD.

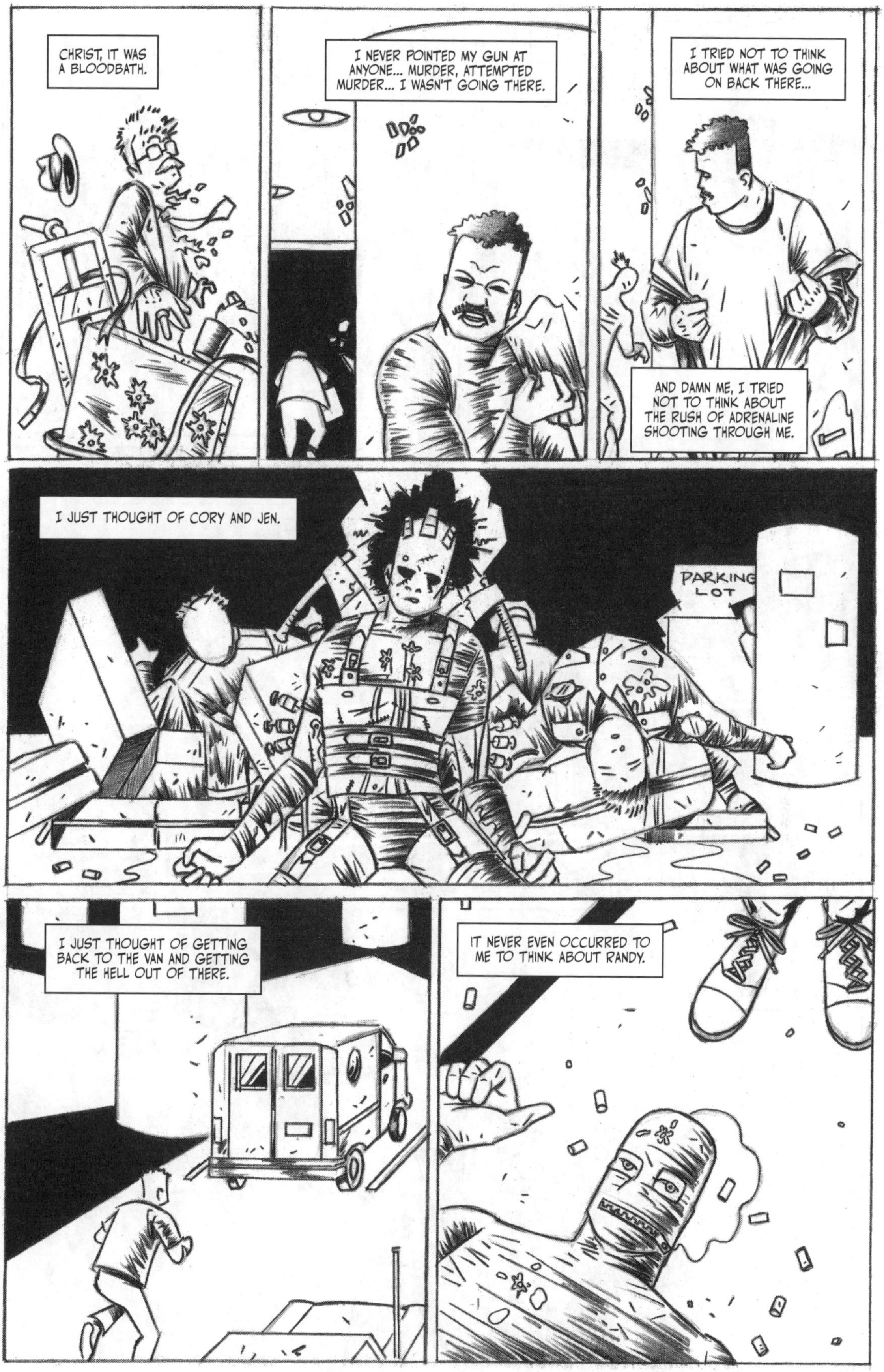
CHRIST, IT WAS A BLOODBATH.
I NEVER POINTED MY GUN AT ANYONE... MURDER, ATTEMPTED MURDER... I WASN'T GOING THERE.
I TRIED NOT TO THINK ABOUT WHAT WAS GOING ON BACK THERE...
AND DAMN ME, I TRIED NOT TO THINK ABOUT THE RUSH OF ADRENALINE SHOOTING THROUGH ME.
I JUST THOUGHT OF CORY AND JEN.
PARKING LOT
I JUST THOUGHT OF GETTING BACK TO THE VAN AND GETTING THE HELL OUT OF THERE.
IT NEVER EVEN OCCURRED TO ME TO THINK ABOUT RANDY.

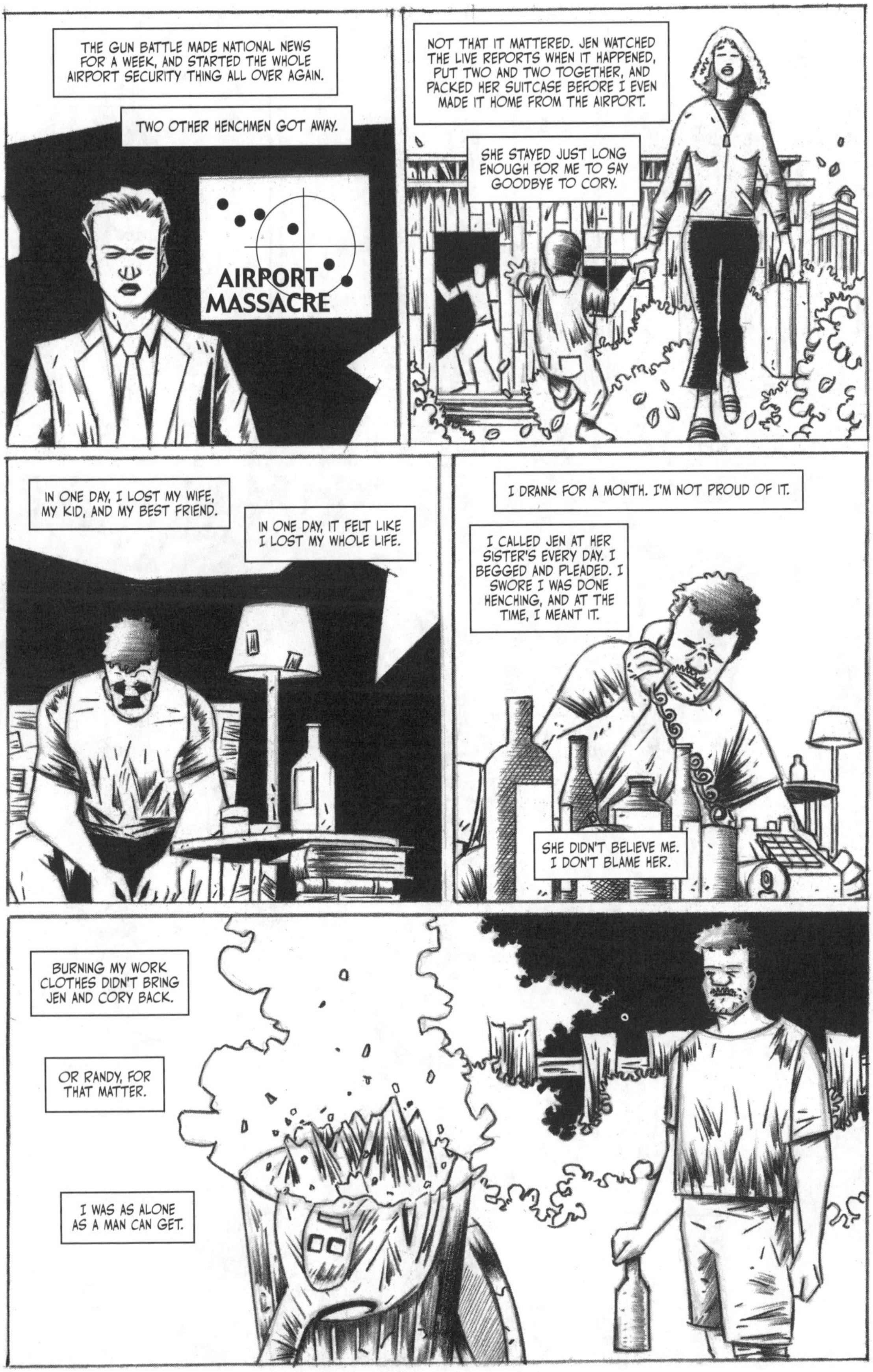
THE GUN BATTLE MADE NATIONAL NEWS FOR A WEEK, AND STARTED THE WHOLE AIRPORT SECURITY THING ALL OVER AGAIN.
TWO OTHER HENCHMEN GOT AWAY.
AIRPORT MASSACRE
NOT THAT IT MATTERED. JEN WATCHED THE LIVE REPORTS WHEN IT HAPPENED, PUT TWO AND TWO TOGETHER, AND PACKED HER SUITCASE BEFORE I EVEN MADE IT HOME FROM THE AIRPORT.
SHE STAYED JUST LONG ENOUGH FOR ME TO SAY GOODBYE TO CORY.
IN ONE DAY, I LOST MY WIFE, MY KID, AND MY BEST FRIEND.
IN ONE DAY, IT FELT LIKE I LOST MY WHOLE LIFE.
I DRANK FOR A MONTH. I'M NOT PROUD OF IT.
I CALLED JEN AT HER SISTER'S EVERY DAY. I BEGGED AND PLEADED. I SWORE I WAS DONE HENCHING, AND AT THE TIME, I MEANT IT.
SHE DIDN'T BELIEVE ME. I DON'T BLAME HER.
BURNING MY WORK CLOTHES DIDN'T BRING JEN AND CORY BACK.
OR RANDY, FOR THAT MATTER.
I WAS AS ALONE AS A MAN CAN GET.

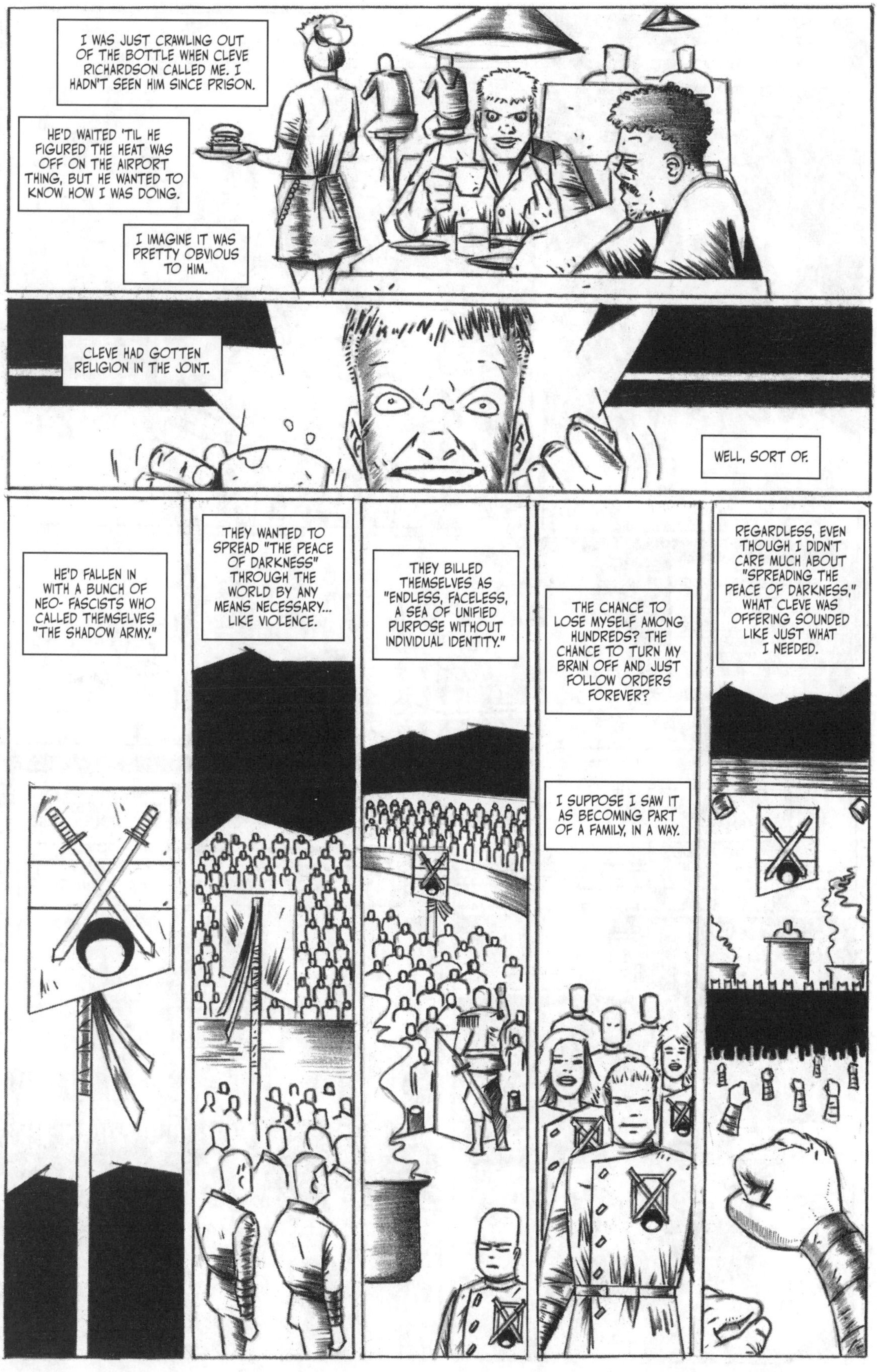
I WAS JUST CRAWLING OUT OF THE BOTTLE WHEN CLEVE RICHARDSON CALLED ME. I HADN'T SEEN HIM SINCE PRISON.
HE'D WAITED 'TIL HE FIGURED THE HEAT WAS OFF ON THE AIRPORT THING, BUT HE WANTED TO KNOW HOW I WAS DOING.
I IMAGINE IT WAS PRETTY OBVIOUS TO HIM.
CLEVE HAD GOTTEN RELIGION IN THE JOINT.
WELL, SORT OF.
HE'D FALLEN IN WITH A BUNCH OF NEO- FASCISTS WHO CALLED THEMSELVES "THE SHADOW ARMY."
THEY WANTED TO SPREAD "THE PEACE OF DARKNESS" THROUGH THE WORLD BY ANY MEANS NECESSARY... LIKE VIOLENCE.
THEY BILLED THEMSELVES AS "ENDLESS, FACELESS, A SEA OF UNIFIED PURPOSE WITHOUT INDIVIDUAL IDENTITY."
THE CHANCE TO LOSE MYSELF AMONG HUNDREDS? THE CHANCE TO TURN MY BRAIN OFF AND JUST FOLLOW ORDERS FOREVER?
I SUPPOSE I SAW IT AS BECOMING PART OF A FAMILY, IN A WAY.
REGARDLESS, EVEN THOUGH I DIDN'T CARE MUCH ABOUT "SPREADING THE PEACE OF DARKNESS," WHAT CLEVE WAS OFFERING SOUNDED LIKE JUST WHAT I NEEDED.

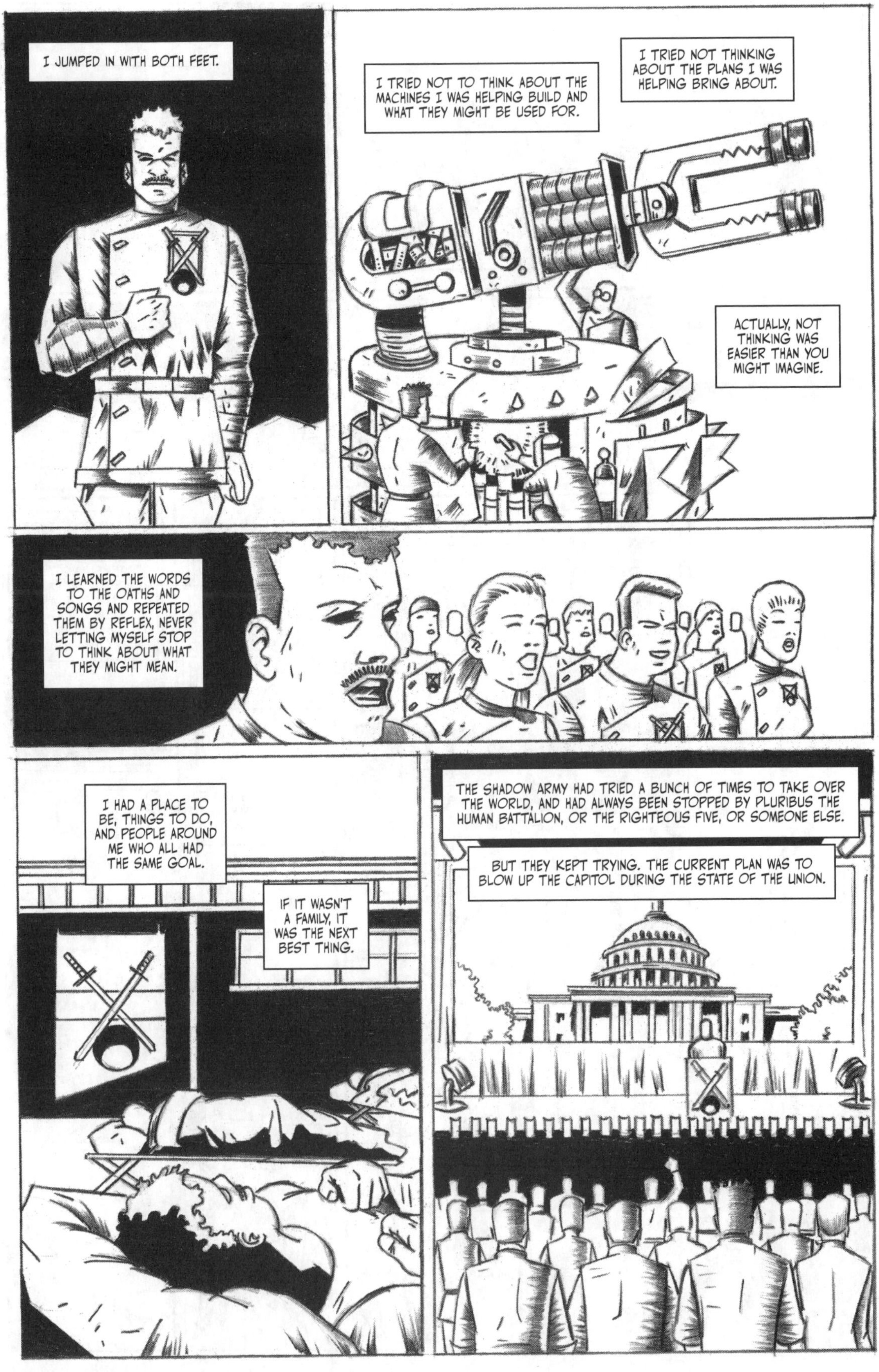
I JUMPED IN WITH BOTH FEET.
I TRIED NOT TO THINK ABOUT THE MACHINES I WAS HELPING BUILD AND WHAT THEY MIGHT BE USED FOR.
I TRIED NOT THINKING ABOUT THE PLANS I WAS HELPING BRING ABOUT.
ACTUALLY, NOT THINKING WAS EASIER THAN YOU MIGHT IMAGINE.
I LEARNED THE WORDS TO THE OATHS AND SONGS AND REPEATED THEM BY REFLEX, NEVER LETTING MYSELF STOP TO THINK ABOUT WHAT THEY MIGHT MEAN.
I HAD A PLACE TO BE, THINGS TO DO, AND PEOPLE AROUND ME WHO ALL HAD THE SAME GOAL.
IF IT WASN'T A FAMILY, IT WAS THE NEXT BEST THING.
THE SHADOW ARMY HAD TRIED A BUNCH OF TIMES TO TAKE OVER THE WORLD, AND HAD ALWAYS BEEN STOPPED BY PLURIBUS THE HUMAN BATTALION, OR THE RIGHTEOUS FIVE, OR SOMEONE ELSE.
BUT THEY KEPT TRYING. THE CURRENT PLAN WAS TO BLOW UP THE CAPITOL DURING THE STATE OF THE UNION.

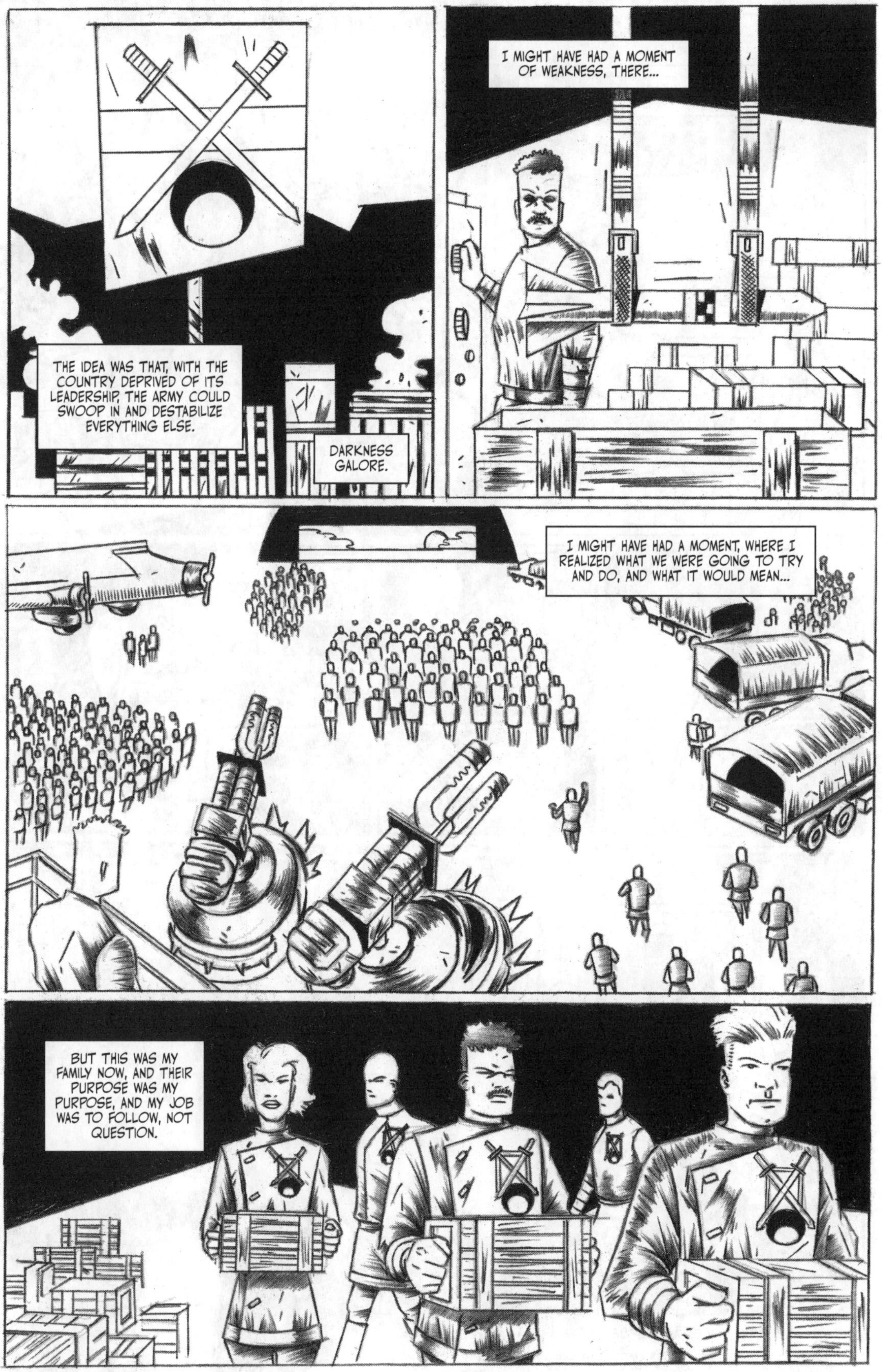
THE IDEA WAS THAT, WITH THE COUNTRY DEPRIVED OF ITS LEADERSHIP, THE ARMY COULD SWOOP IN AND DESTABILIZE EVERYTHING ELSE.
DARKNESS GALORE.
I MIGHT HAVE HAD A MOMENT OF WEAKNESS, THERE...
I MIGHT HAVE HAD A MOMENT, WHERE I REALIZED WHAT WE WERE GOING TO TRY AND DO, AND WHAT IT WOULD MEAN...
BUT THIS WAS MY FAMILY NOW, AND THEIR PURPOSE WAS MY PURPOSE, AND MY JOB WAS TO FOLLOW, NOT QUESTION.

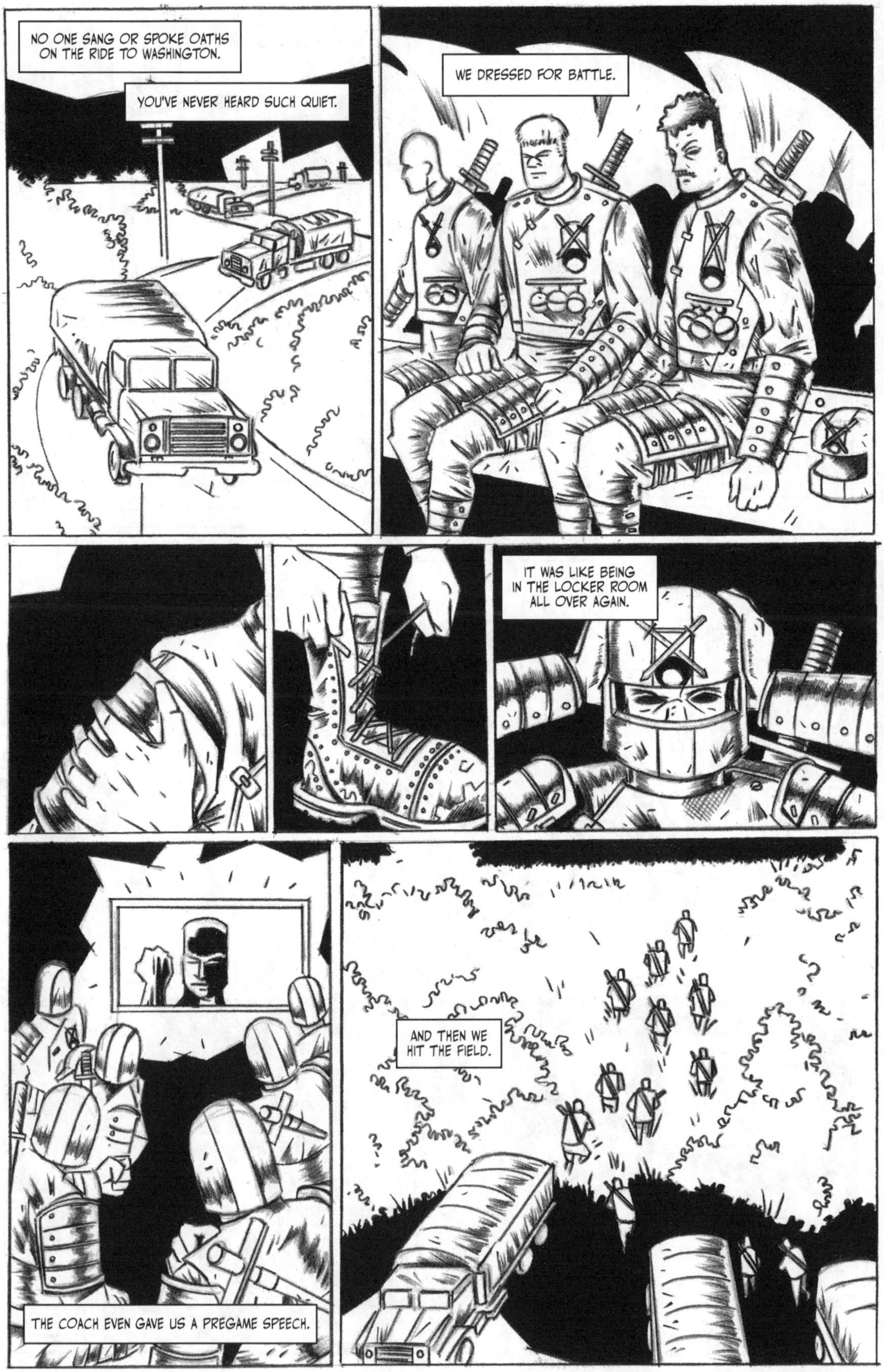
NO ONE SANG OR SPOKE OATHS ON THE RIDE TO WASHINGTON.
YOU'VE NEVER HEARD SUCH QUIET.
WE DRESSED FOR BATTLE.
IT WAS LIKE BEING IN THE LOCKER ROOM ALL OVER AGAIN.
THE COACH EVEN GAVE US A PREGAME SPEECH.
AND THEN WE HIT THE FIELD.

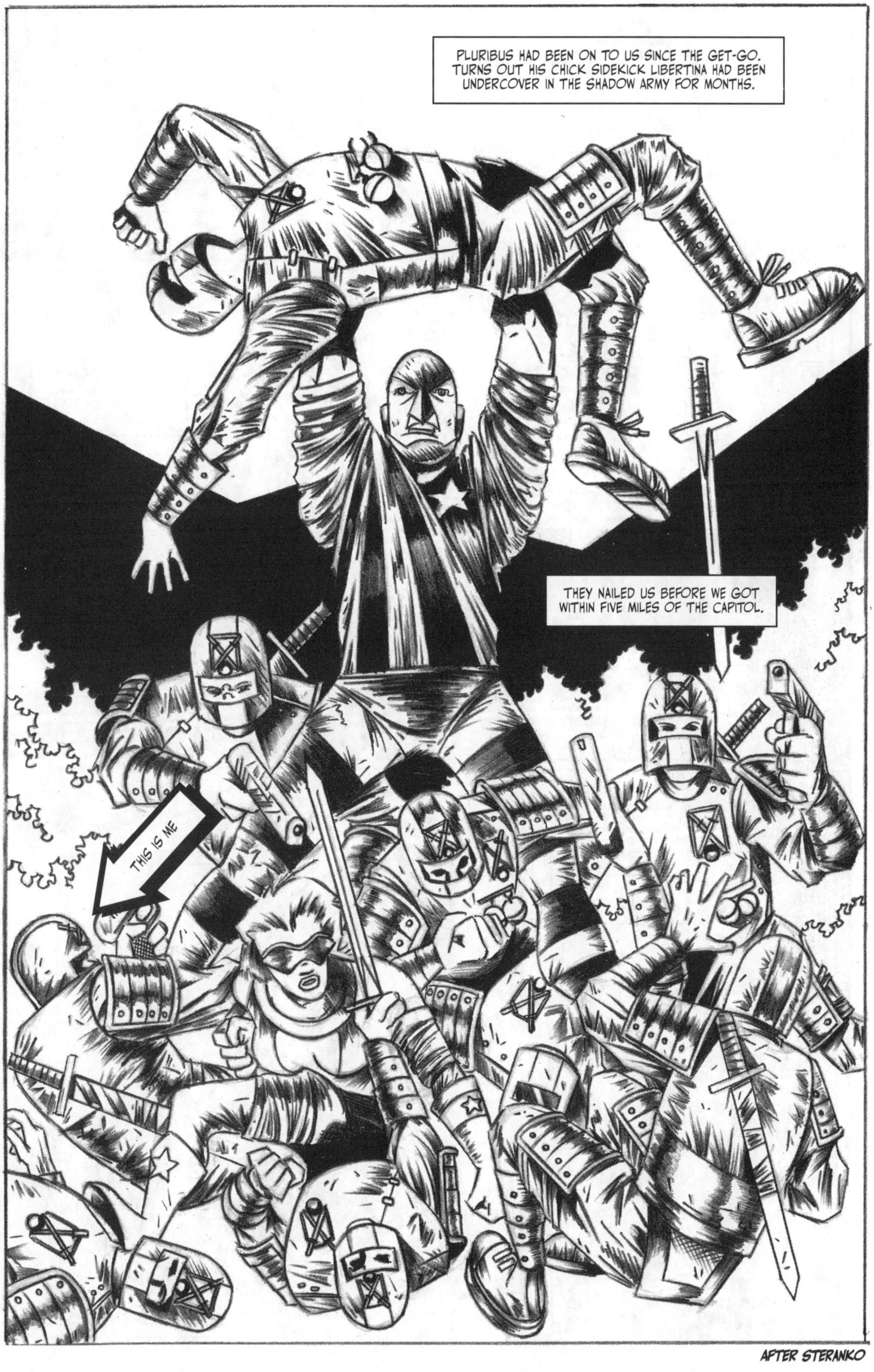
PLURIBUS HAD BEEN ON TO US SINCE THE GET-GO. TURNS OUT HIS CHICK SIDEKICK LIBERTINA HAD BEEN UNDERCOVER IN THE SHADOW ARMY FOR MONTHS.
THEY NAILED US BEFORE WE GOT WITHIN FIVE MILES OF THE CAPITOL.
THIS IS ME

AFTER STERANKO

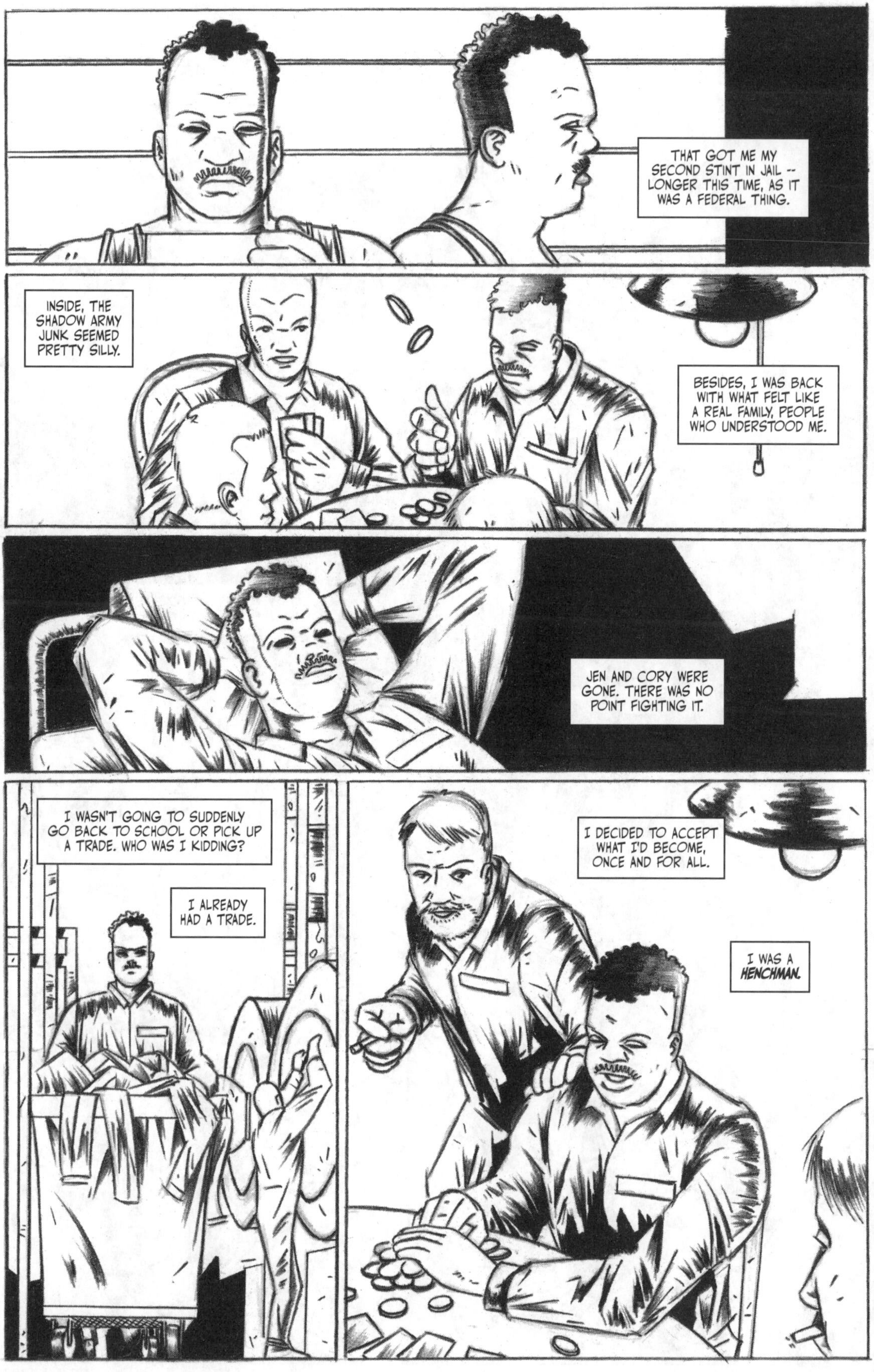
THAT GOT ME MY SECOND STINT IN JAIL -- LONGER THIS TIME, AS IT WAS A FEDERAL THING.
INSIDE, THE SHADOW ARMY JUNK SEEMED PRETTY SILLY.
BESIDES, I WAS BACK WITH WHAT FELT LIKE A REAL FAMILY, PEOPLE WHO UNDERSTOOD ME.
JEN AND CORY WERE GONE. THERE WAS NO POINT FIGHTING IT.
I WASN'T GOING TO SUDDENLY GO BACK TO SCHOOL OR PICK UP A TRADE. WHO WAS I KIDDING?
I ALREADY HAD A TRADE.
I DECIDED TO ACCEPT WHAT I'D BECOME, ONCE AND FOR ALL.
I WAS A ***HENCHMAN.***

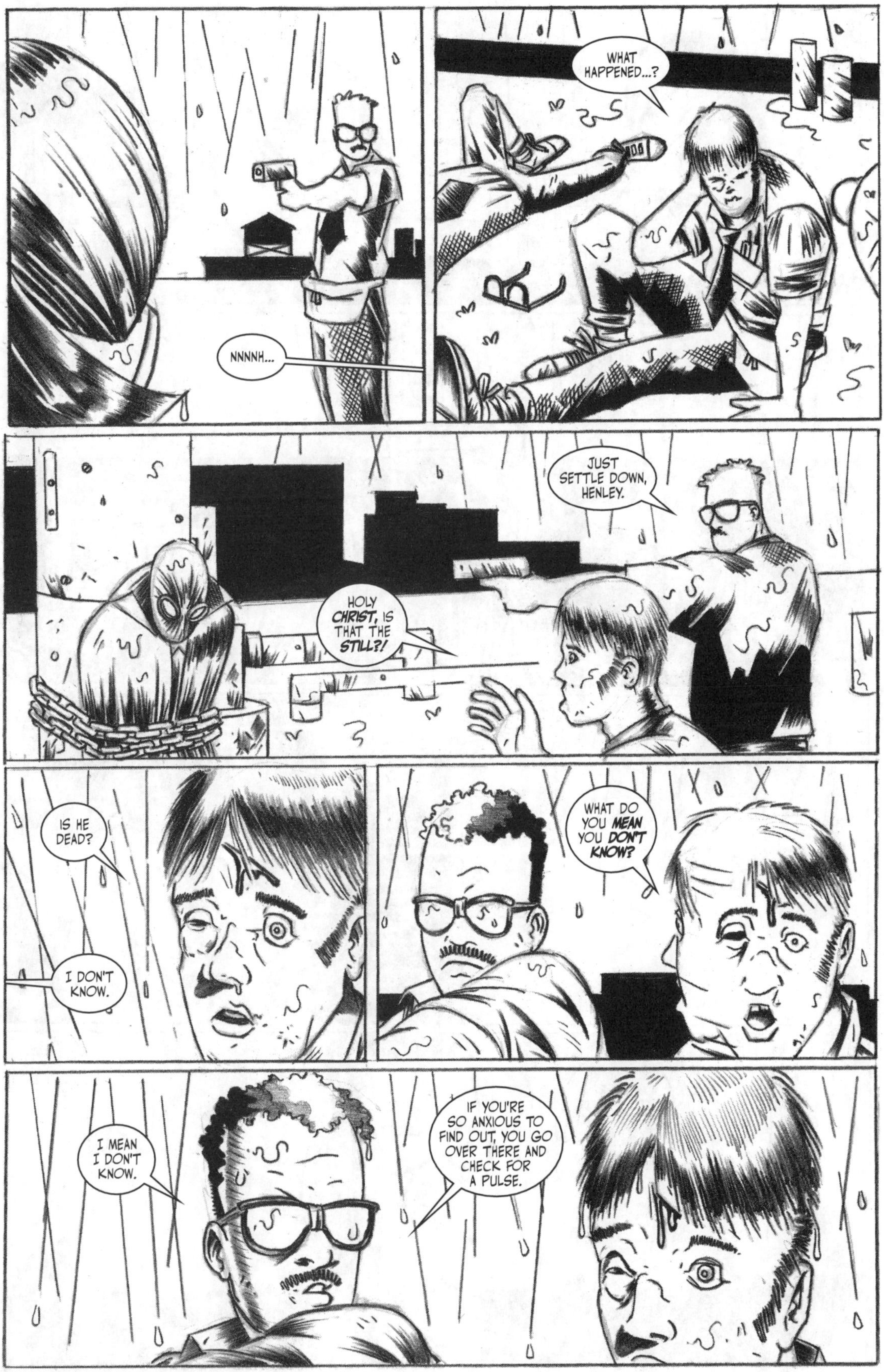
NNNNH...
WHAT HAPPENED...?
JUST SETTLE DOWN, HENLEY.
HOLY CHRIST, IS THAT THE STILL?!
IS HE DEAD?
I DON'T KNOW.
WHAT DO YOU MEAN YOU DON'T KNOW?
I MEAN I DON'T KNOW.
IF YOU'RE SO ANXIOUS TO FIND OUT, YOU GO OVER THERE AND CHECK FOR A PULSE.

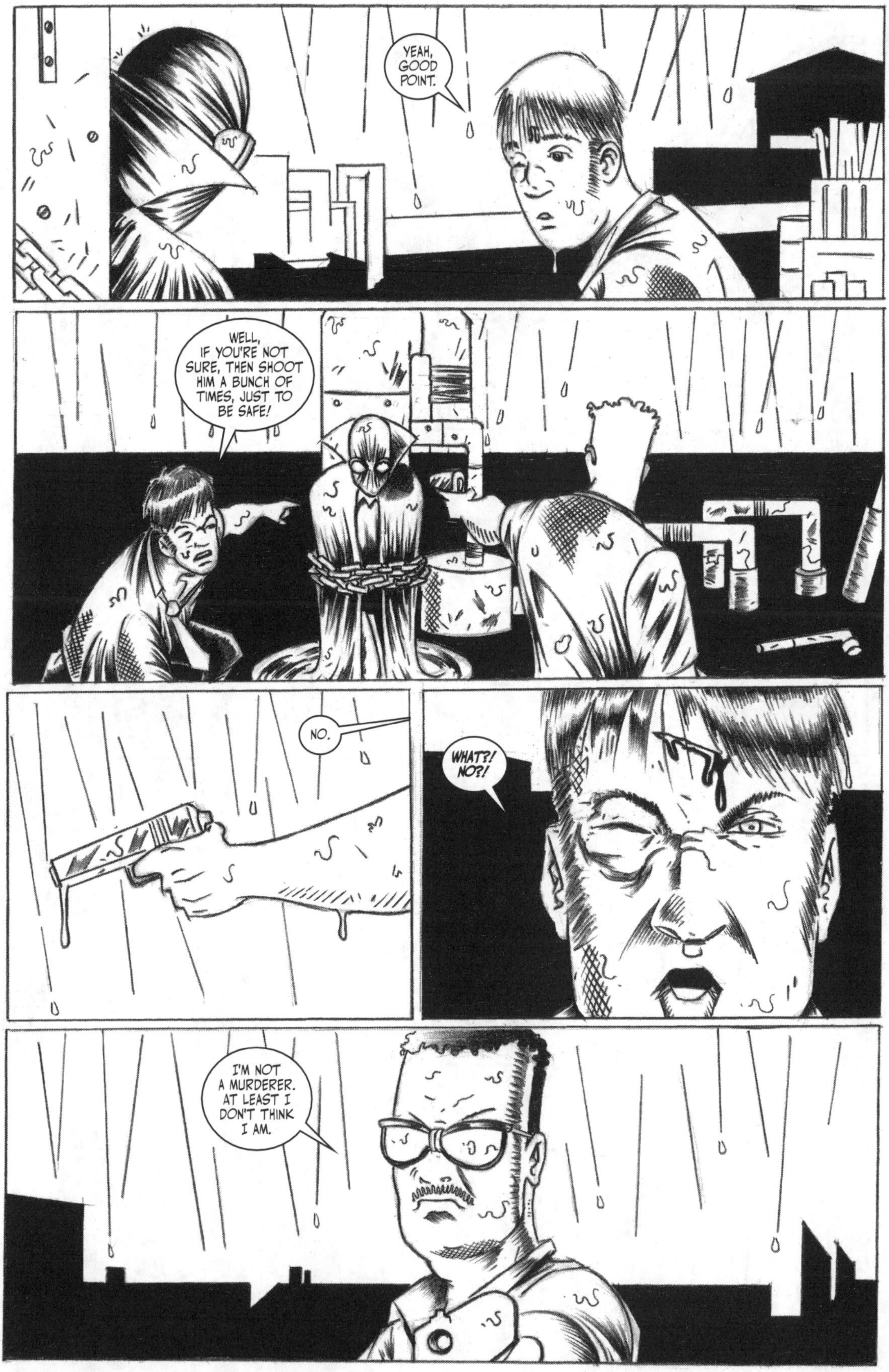
YEAH, GOOD POINT.
WELL, IF YOU'RE NOT SURE, THEN SHOOT HIM A BUNCH OF TIMES, JUST TO BE SAFE!
NO.
WHAT?! NO?!
I'M NOT A MURDERER. AT LEAST I DON'T THINK I AM.

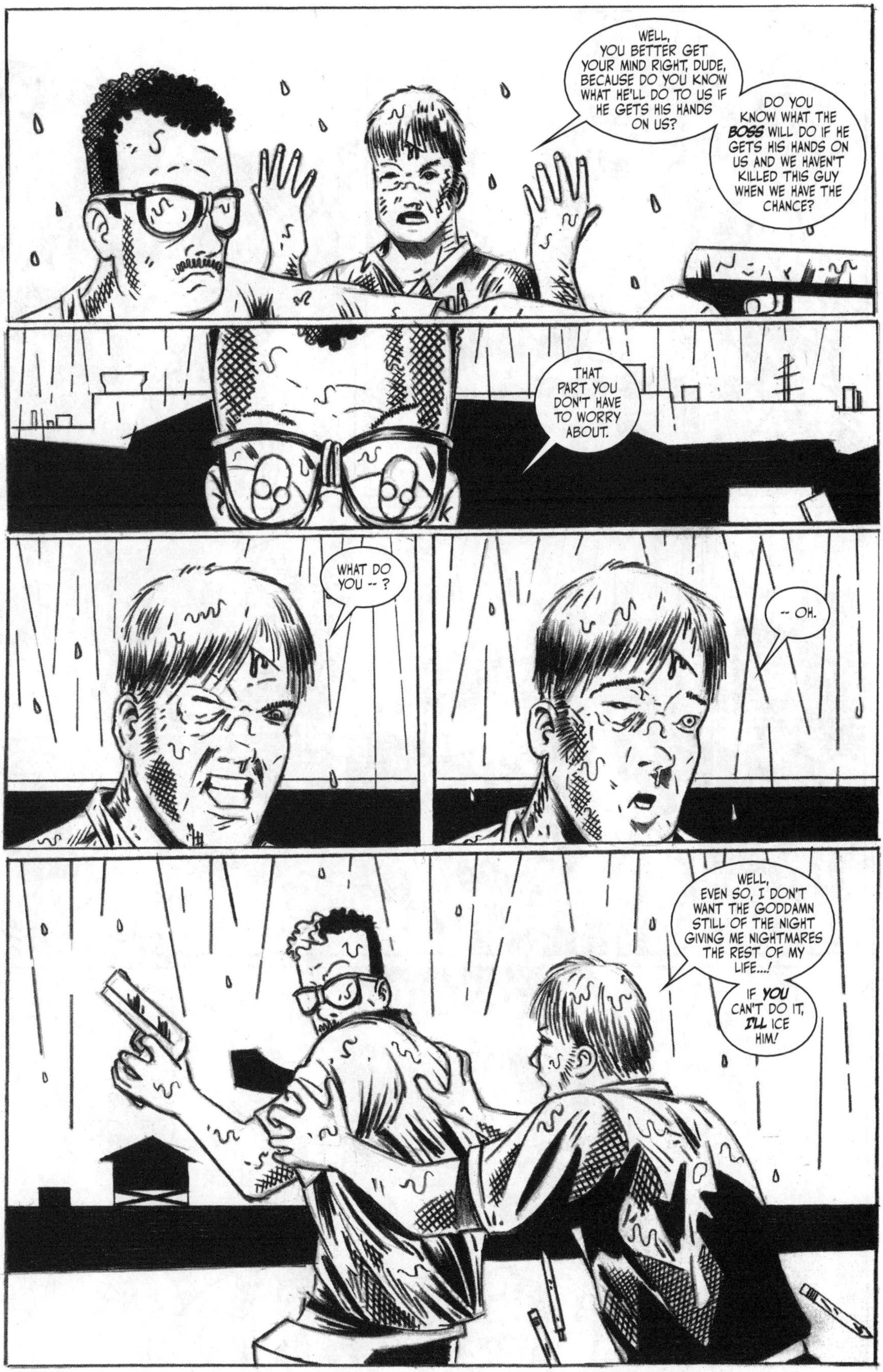
WELL, YOU BETTER GET YOUR MIND RIGHT, DUDE, BECAUSE DO YOU KNOW WHAT HE'LL DO TO US IF HE GETS HIS HANDS ON US?
DO YOU KNOW WHAT THE BOSS WILL DO IF HE GETS HIS HANDS ON US AND WE HAVEN'T KILLED THIS GUY WHEN WE HAVE THE CHANCE?
THAT PART YOU DON'T HAVE TO WORRY ABOUT.
WHAT DO YOU -- ?
-- OH.
WELL, EVEN SO, I DON'T WANT THE GODDAMN STILL OF THE NIGHT GIVING ME NIGHTMARES THE REST OF MY LIFE...!
IF YOU CAN'T DO IT, I'LL ICE HIM!

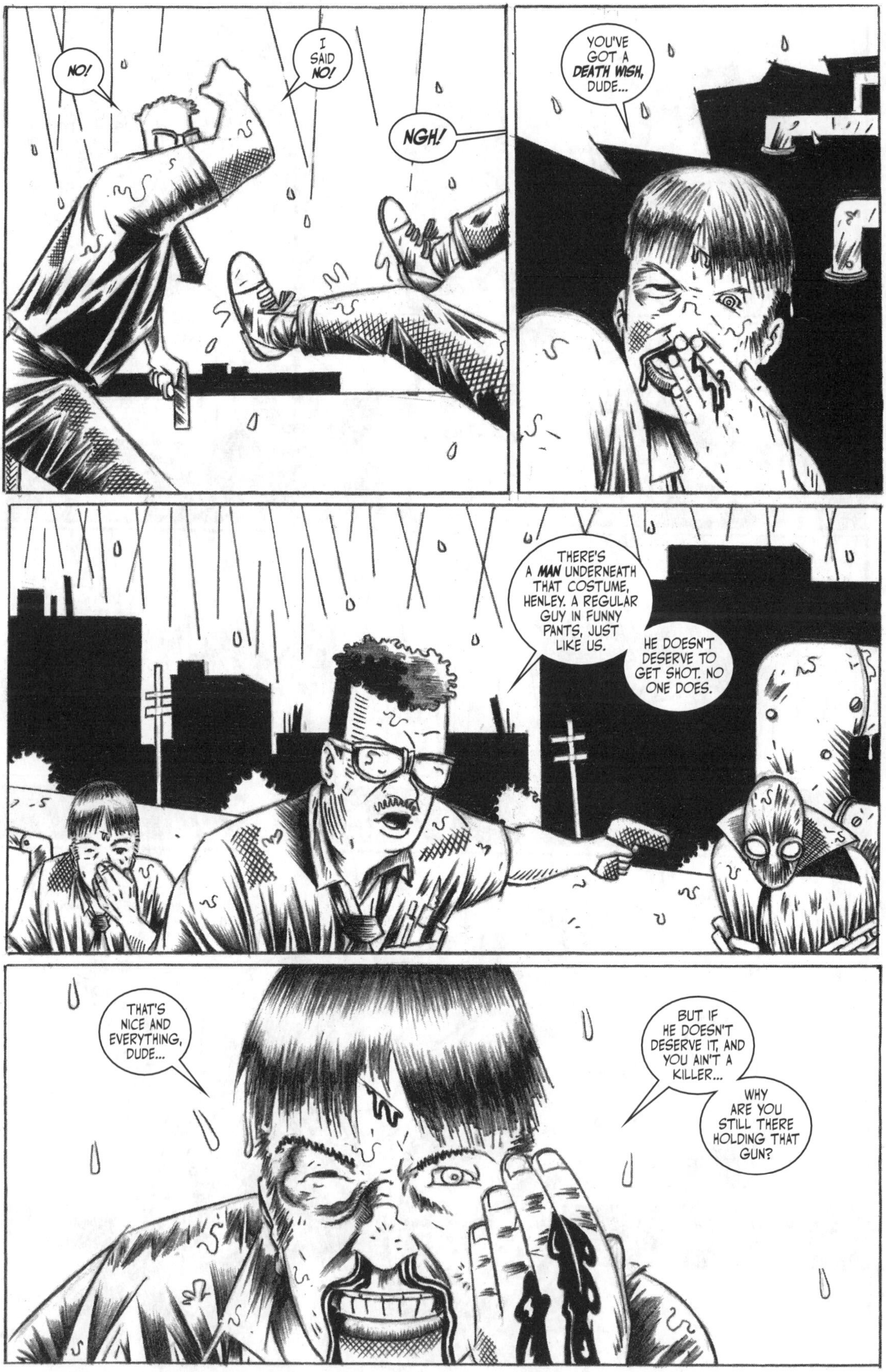
NO!
I SAID NO!
NGH!
YOU'VE GOT A **DEATH WISH,** DUDE...
THERE'S A **MAN** UNDERNEATH THAT COSTUME, HENLEY. A REGULAR GUY IN FUNNY PANTS, JUST LIKE US.
HE DOESN'T DESERVE TO GET SHOT. NO ONE DOES.
THAT'S NICE AND EVERYTHING, DUDE...
BUT IF HE DOESN'T DESERVE IT, AND YOU AIN'T A KILLER...
WHY ARE YOU STILL THERE HOLDING THAT GUN?

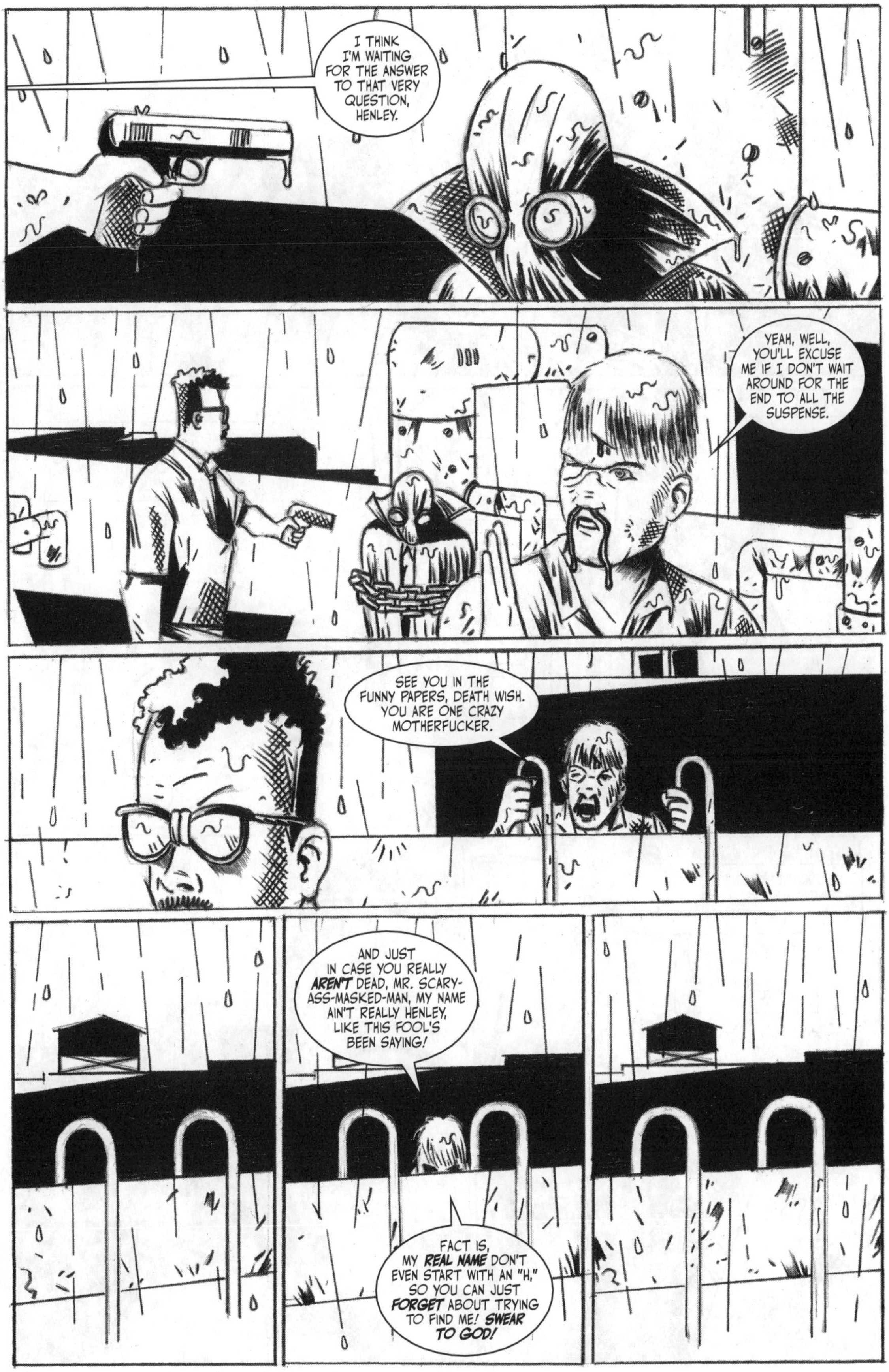
I THINK I'M WAITING FOR THE ANSWER TO THAT VERY QUESTION, HENLEY.
YEAH, WELL, YOU'LL EXCUSE ME IF I DON'T WAIT AROUND FOR THE END TO ALL THE SUSPENSE.
SEE YOU IN THE FUNNY PAPERS, DEATH WISH. YOU ARE ONE CRAZY MOTHERFUCKER.
AND JUST IN CASE YOU REALLY **AREN'T** DEAD, MR. SCARY-ASS-MASKED-MAN, MY NAME AIN'T REALLY HENLEY, LIKE THIS FOOL'S BEEN SAYING!
FACT IS, MY **REAL NAME** DON'T EVEN START WITH AN "H," SO YOU CAN JUST **FORGET** ABOUT TRYING TO FIND ME! **SWEAR TO GOD!**

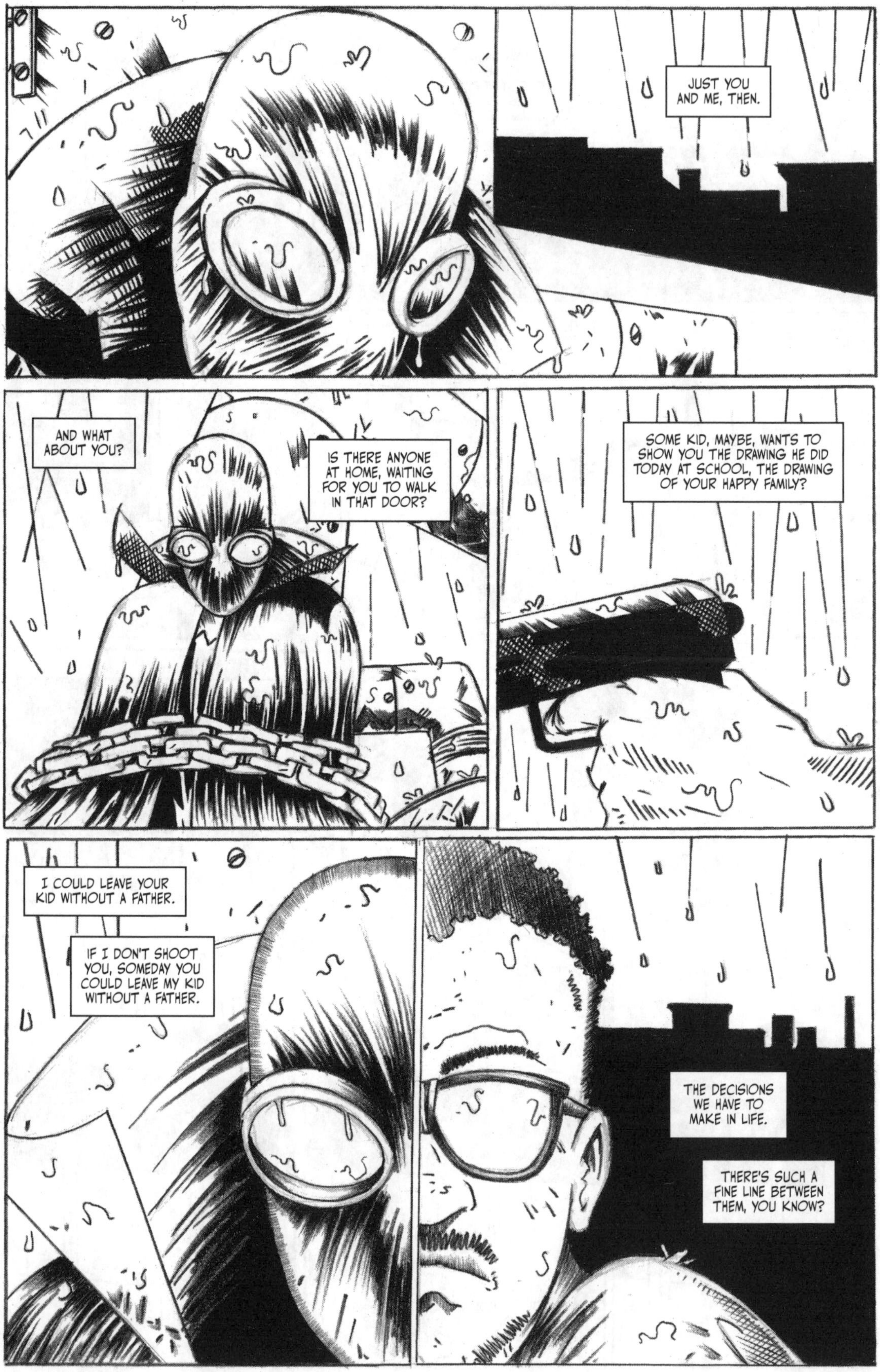
JUST YOU AND ME, THEN.
AND WHAT ABOUT YOU?
IS THERE ANYONE AT HOME, WAITING FOR YOU TO WALK IN THAT DOOR?
SOME KID, MAYBE, WANTS TO SHOW YOU THE DRAWING HE DID TODAY AT SCHOOL, THE DRAWING OF YOUR HAPPY FAMILY?
I COULD LEAVE YOUR KID WITHOUT A FATHER.
IF I DON'T SHOOT YOU, SOMEDAY YOU COULD LEAVE MY KID WITHOUT A FATHER.
THE DECISIONS WE HAVE TO MAKE IN LIFE.
THERE'S SUCH A FINE LINE BETWEEN THEM, YOU KNOW?

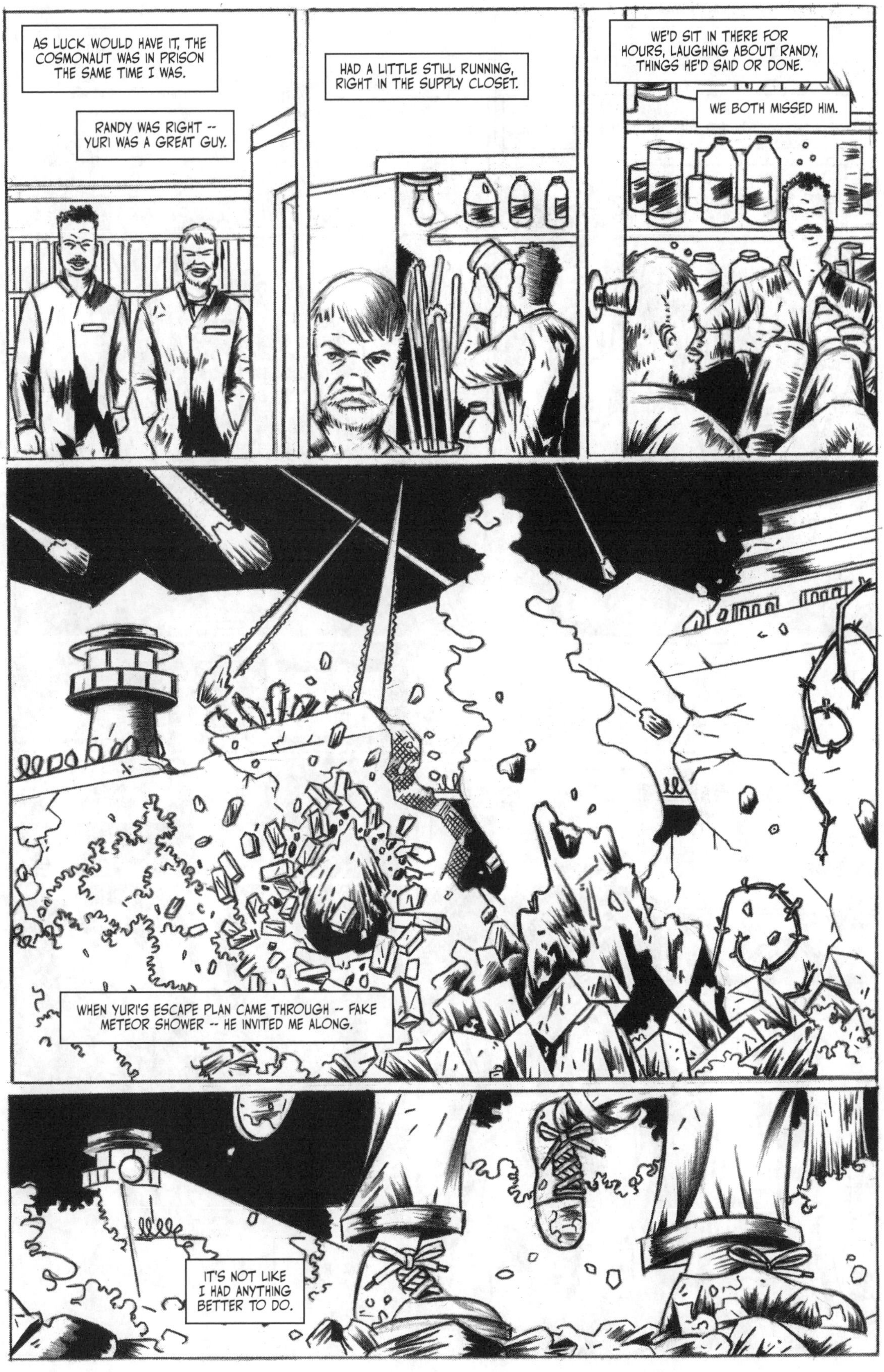
AS LUCK WOULD HAVE IT, THE COSMONAUT WAS IN PRISON THE SAME TIME I WAS.
RANDY WAS RIGHT -- YURI WAS A GREAT GUY.
HAD A LITTLE STILL RUNNING, RIGHT IN THE SUPPLY CLOSET.
WE'D SIT IN THERE FOR HOURS, LAUGHING ABOUT RANDY, THINGS HE'D SAID OR DONE.
WE BOTH MISSED HIM.
WHEN YURI'S ESCAPE PLAN CAME THROUGH -- FAKE METEOR SHOWER -- HE INVITED ME ALONG.
IT'S NOT LIKE I HAD ANYTHING BETTER TO DO.

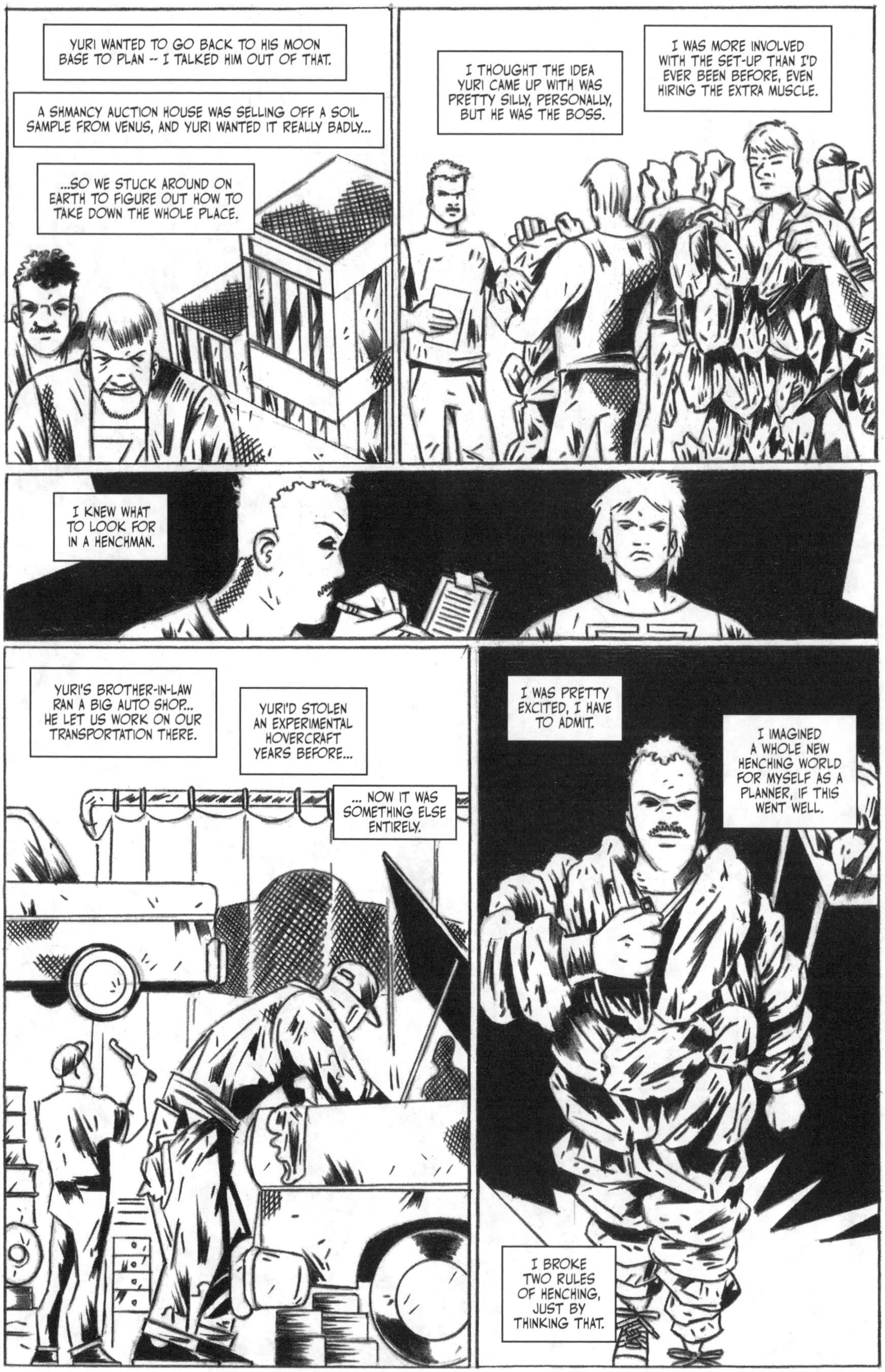
YURI WANTED TO GO BACK TO HIS MOON BASE TO PLAN -- I TALKED HIM OUT OF THAT.
A SHMANCY AUCTION HOUSE WAS SELLING OFF A SOIL SAMPLE FROM VENUS, AND YURI WANTED IT REALLY BADLY...
...SO WE STUCK AROUND ON EARTH TO FIGURE OUT HOW TO TAKE DOWN THE WHOLE PLACE.
I THOUGHT THE IDEA YURI CAME UP WITH WAS PRETTY SILLY, PERSONALLY, BUT HE WAS THE BOSS.
I WAS MORE INVOLVED WITH THE SET-UP THAN I'D EVER BEEN BEFORE, EVEN HIRING THE EXTRA MUSCLE.
I KNEW WHAT TO LOOK FOR IN A HENCHMAN.
YURI'S BROTHER-IN-LAW RAN A BIG AUTO SHOP... HE LET US WORK ON OUR TRANSPORTATION THERE.
YURI'D STOLEN AN EXPERIMENTAL HOVERCRAFT YEARS BEFORE...
... NOW IT WAS SOMETHING ELSE ENTIRELY.
I WAS PRETTY EXCITED, I HAVE TO ADMIT.
I IMAGINED A WHOLE NEW HENCHING WORLD FOR MYSELF AS A PLANNER, IF THIS WENT WELL.
I BROKE TWO RULES OF HENCHING, JUST BY THINKING THAT.

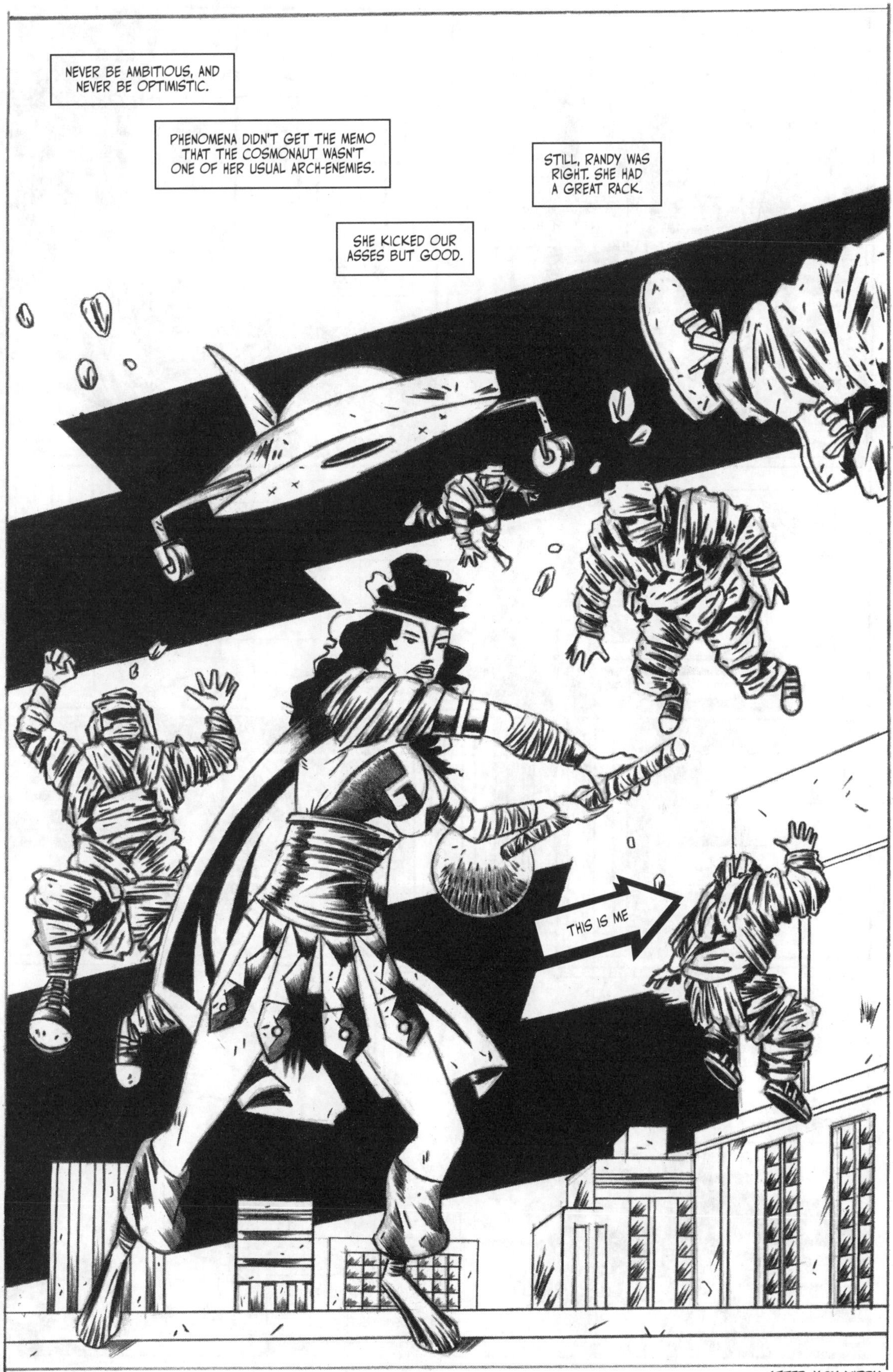

AFTER JACK KIRBY

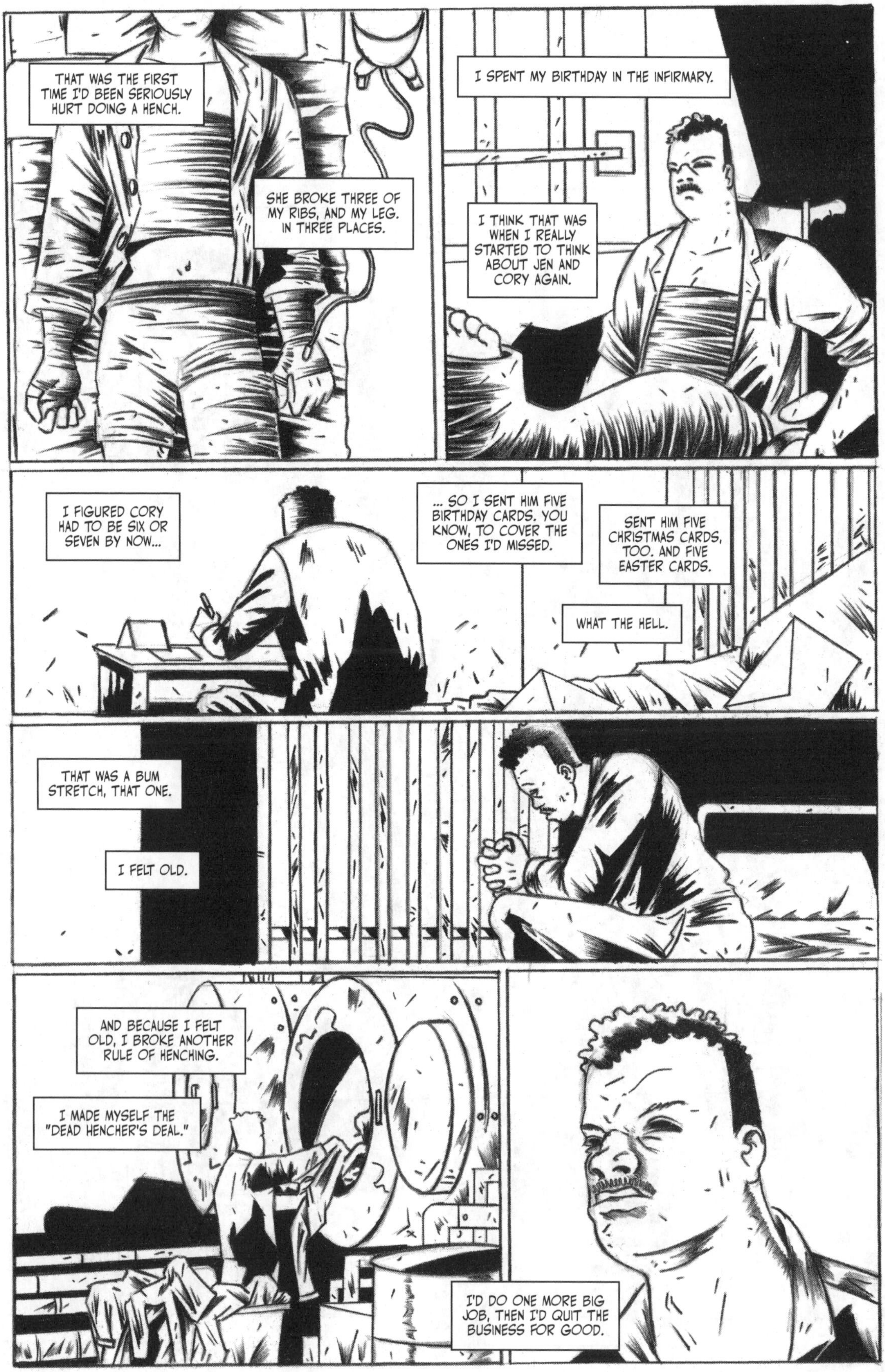
THAT WAS THE FIRST TIME I'D BEEN SERIOUSLY HURT DOING A HENCH.
SHE BROKE THREE OF MY RIBS, AND MY LEG. IN THREE PLACES.
I SPENT MY BIRTHDAY IN THE INFIRMARY.
I THINK THAT WAS WHEN I REALLY STARTED TO THINK ABOUT JEN AND CORY AGAIN.
I FIGURED CORY HAD TO BE SIX OR SEVEN BY NOW...
... SO I SENT HIM FIVE BIRTHDAY CARDS. YOU KNOW, TO COVER THE ONES I'D MISSED.
SENT HIM FIVE CHRISTMAS CARDS, TOO. AND FIVE EASTER CARDS.
WHAT THE HELL.
THAT WAS A BUM STRETCH, THAT ONE.
I FELT OLD.
AND BECAUSE I FELT OLD, I BROKE ANOTHER RULE OF HENCHING.
I MADE MYSELF THE "DEAD HENCHER'S DEAL."
I'D DO ONE MORE BIG JOB, THEN I'D QUIT THE BUSINESS FOR GOOD.

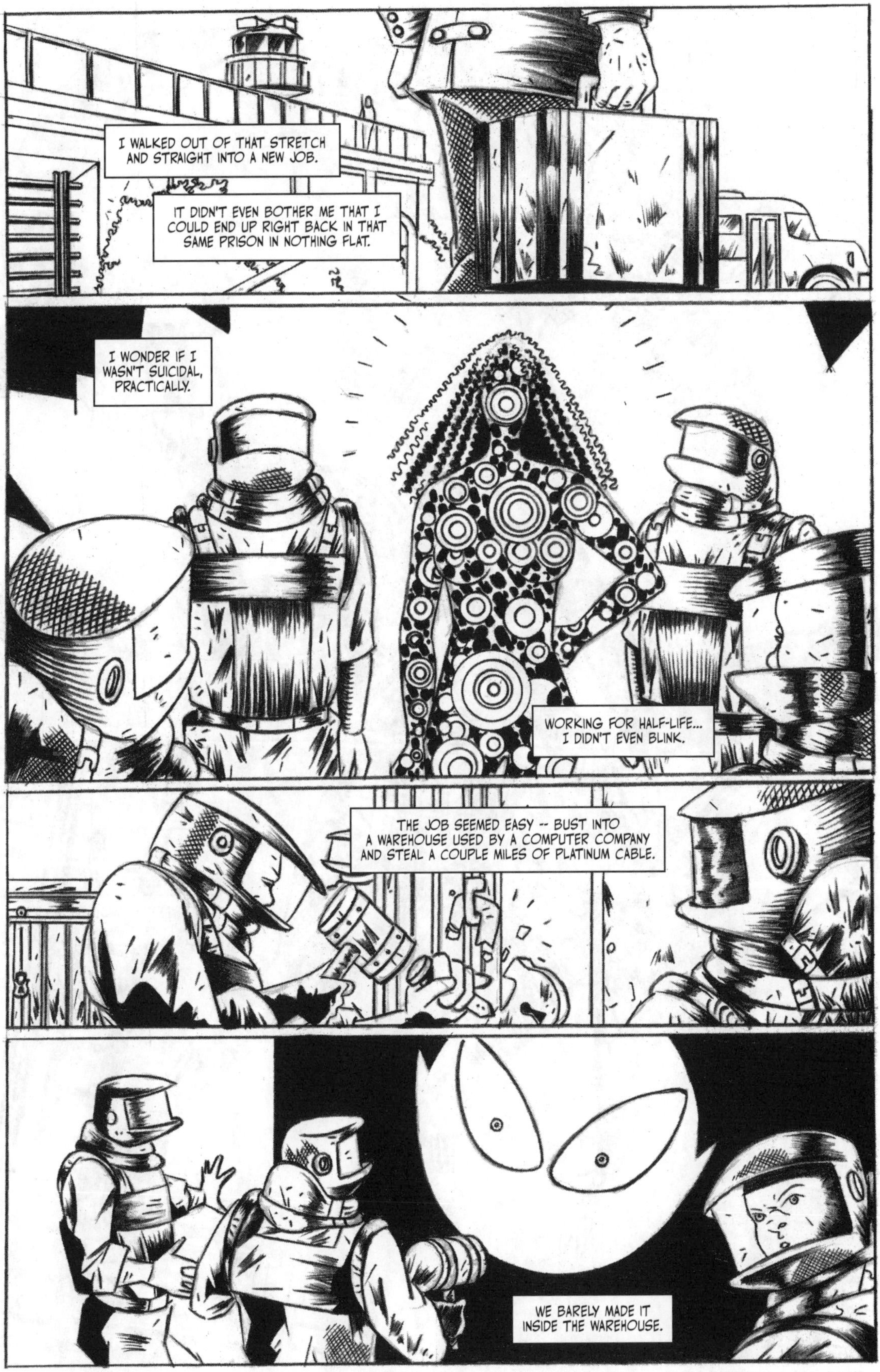
I WALKED OUT OF THAT STRETCH AND STRAIGHT INTO A NEW JOB.
IT DIDN'T EVEN BOTHER ME THAT I COULD END UP RIGHT BACK IN THAT SAME PRISON IN NOTHING FLAT.
I WONDER IF I WASN'T SUICIDAL, PRACTICALLY.
WORKING FOR HALF-LIFE... I DIDN'T EVEN BLINK.
THE JOB SEEMED EASY -- BUST INTO A WAREHOUSE USED BY A COMPUTER COMPANY AND STEAL A COUPLE MILES OF PLATINUM CABLE.
WE BARELY MADE IT INSIDE THE WAREHOUSE.

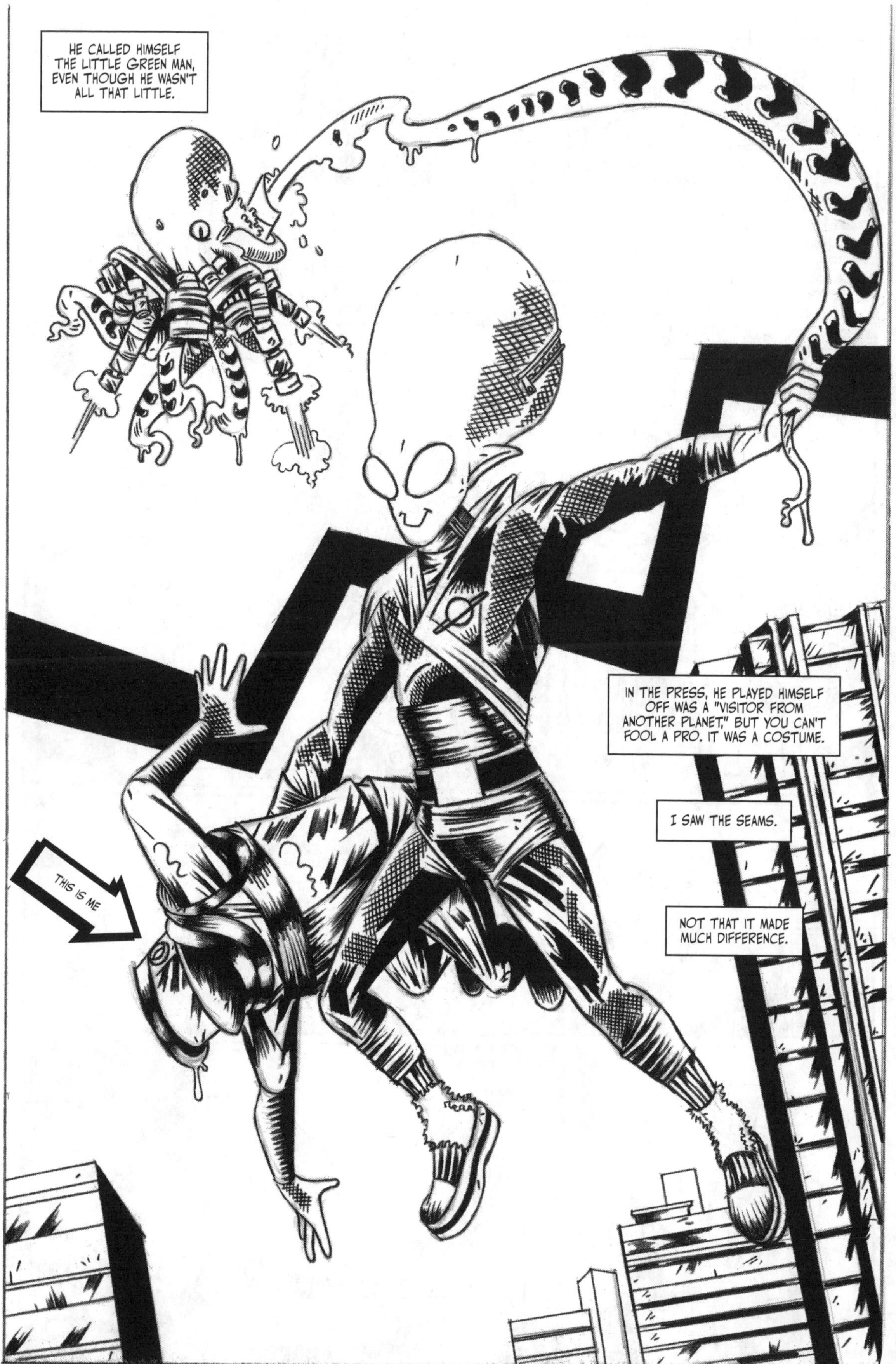
HE CALLED HIMSELF THE LITTLE GREEN MAN, EVEN THOUGH HE WASN'T ALL THAT LITTLE.
IN THE PRESS, HE PLAYED HIMSELF OFF WAS A "VISITOR FROM ANOTHER PLANET," BUT YOU CAN'T FOOL A PRO. IT WAS A COSTUME.
I SAW THE SEAMS.
NOT THAT IT MADE MUCH DIFFERENCE.
THIS IS ME

AFTER JACK KIRBY AND STEVE DITKO

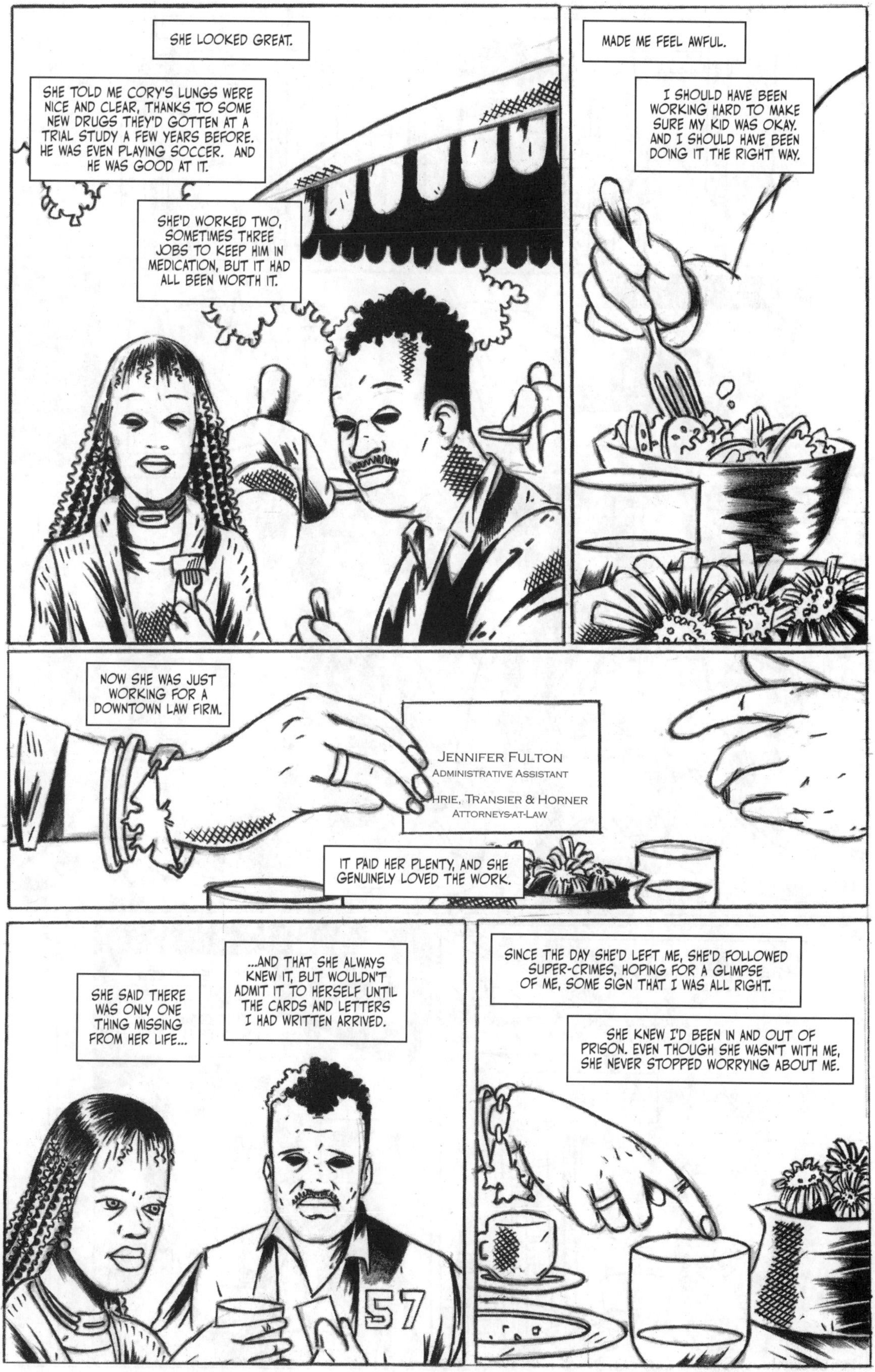
SHE LOOKED GREAT.
SHE TOLD ME CORY'S LUNGS WERE NICE AND CLEAR, THANKS TO SOME NEW DRUGS THEY'D GOTTEN AT A TRIAL STUDY A FEW YEARS BEFORE. HE WAS EVEN PLAYING SOCCER. AND HE WAS GOOD AT IT.
SHE'D WORKED TWO, SOMETIMES THREE JOBS TO KEEP HIM IN MEDICATION, BUT IT HAD ALL BEEN WORTH IT.
MADE ME FEEL AWFUL.
I SHOULD HAVE BEEN WORKING HARD TO MAKE SURE MY KID WAS OKAY. AND I SHOULD HAVE BEEN DOING IT THE RIGHT WAY.
NOW SHE WAS JUST WORKING FOR A DOWNTOWN LAW FIRM.
JENNIFER FULTON
ADMINISTRATIVE ASSISTANT
HRIE, TRANSIER & HORNER
ATTORNEYS-AT-LAW
IT PAID HER PLENTY, AND SHE GENUINELY LOVED THE WORK.
SHE SAID THERE WAS ONLY ONE THING MISSING FROM HER LIFE...
...AND THAT SHE ALWAYS KNEW IT, BUT WOULDN'T ADMIT IT TO HERSELF UNTIL THE CARDS AND LETTERS I HAD WRITTEN ARRIVED.
57
SINCE THE DAY SHE'D LEFT ME, SHE'D FOLLOWED SUPER-CRIMES, HOPING FOR A GLIMPSE OF ME, SOME SIGN THAT I WAS ALL RIGHT.
SHE KNEW I'D BEEN IN AND OUT OF PRISON. EVEN THOUGH SHE WASN'T WITH ME, SHE NEVER STOPPED WORRYING ABOUT ME.

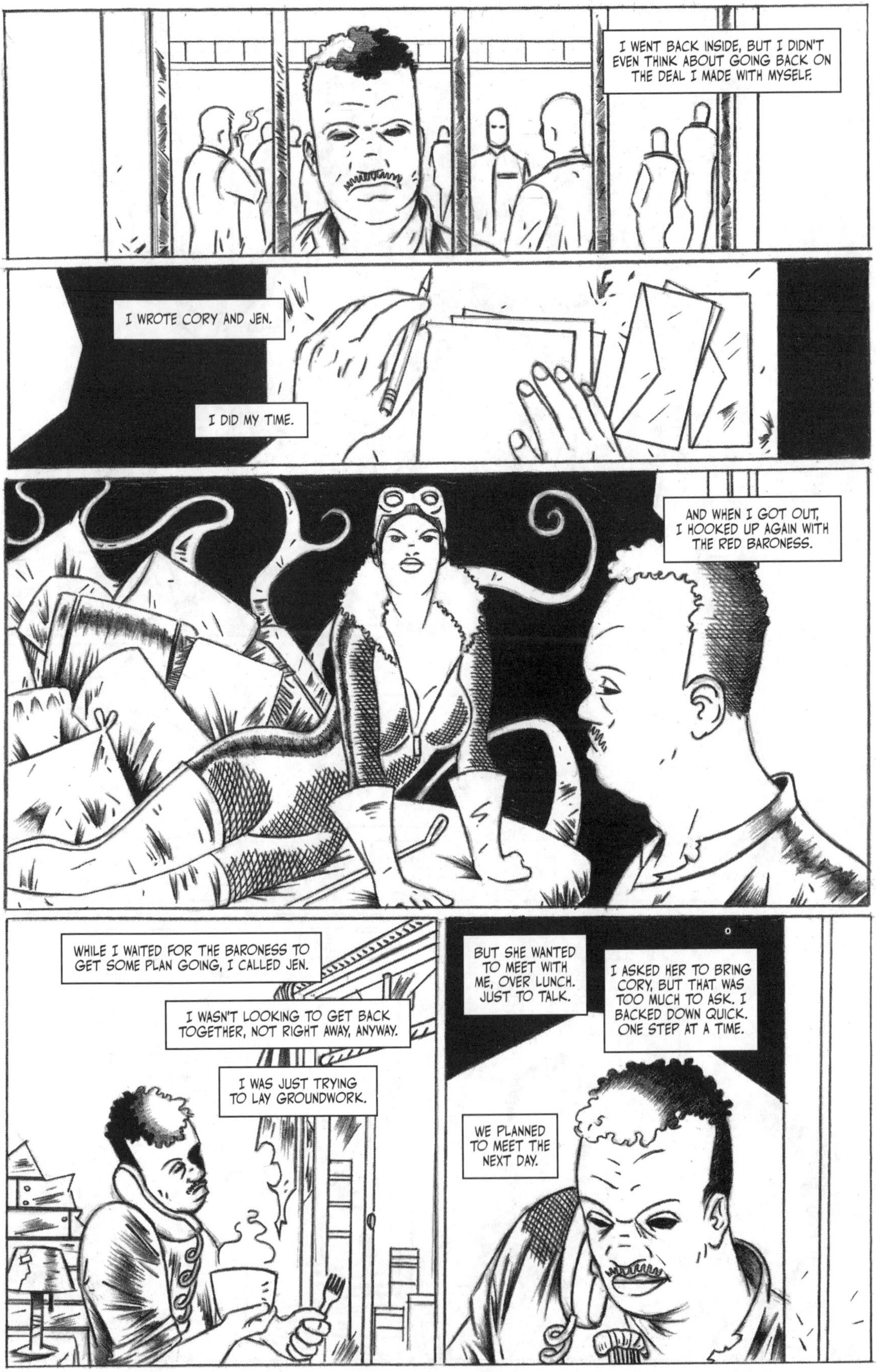
I WENT BACK INSIDE, BUT I DIDN'T EVEN THINK ABOUT GOING BACK ON THE DEAL I MADE WITH MYSELF.
I WROTE CORY AND JEN.
I DID MY TIME.
AND WHEN I GOT OUT, I HOOKED UP AGAIN WITH THE RED BARONESS.
WHILE I WAITED FOR THE BARONESS TO GET SOME PLAN GOING, I CALLED JEN.
I WASN'T LOOKING TO GET BACK TOGETHER, NOT RIGHT AWAY, ANYWAY.
I WAS JUST TRYING TO LAY GROUNDWORK.
BUT SHE WANTED TO MEET WITH ME, OVER LUNCH. JUST TO TALK.
I ASKED HER TO BRING CORY, BUT THAT WAS TOO MUCH TO ASK. I BACKED DOWN QUICK. ONE STEP AT A TIME.
WE PLANNED TO MEET THE NEXT DAY.

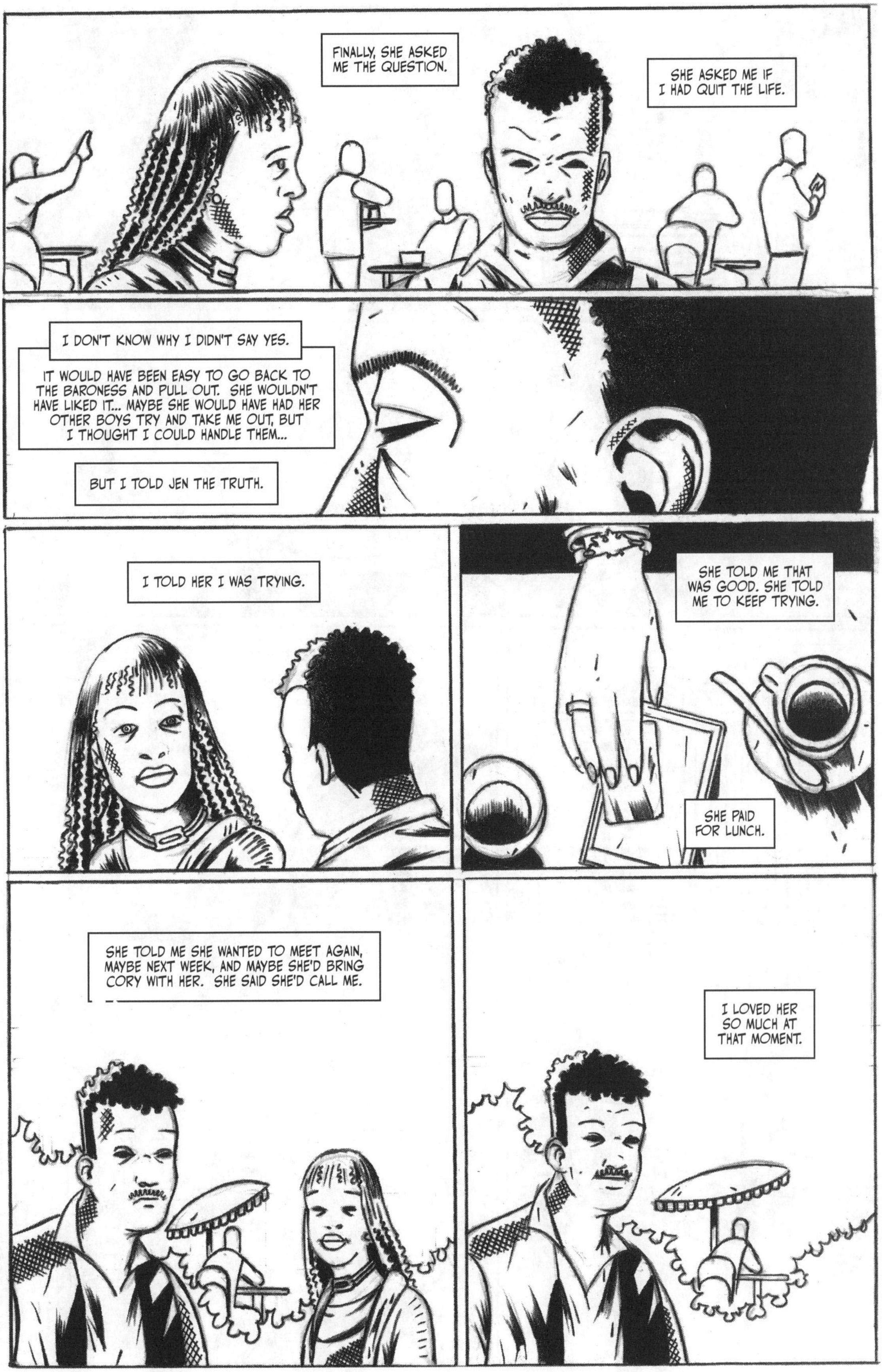
FINALLY, SHE ASKED ME THE QUESTION.
SHE ASKED ME IF I HAD QUIT THE LIFE.
I DON'T KNOW WHY I DIDN'T SAY YES.
IT WOULD HAVE BEEN EASY TO GO BACK TO THE BARONESS AND PULL OUT. SHE WOULDN'T HAVE LIKED IT... MAYBE SHE WOULD HAVE HAD HER OTHER BOYS TRY AND TAKE ME OUT, BUT I THOUGHT I COULD HANDLE THEM...
BUT I TOLD JEN THE TRUTH.
I TOLD HER I WAS TRYING.
SHE TOLD ME THAT WAS GOOD. SHE TOLD ME TO KEEP TRYING.
SHE PAID FOR LUNCH.
SHE TOLD ME SHE WANTED TO MEET AGAIN, MAYBE NEXT WEEK, AND MAYBE SHE'D BRING CORY WITH HER. SHE SAID SHE'D CALL ME.
I LOVED HER SO MUCH AT THAT MOMENT.

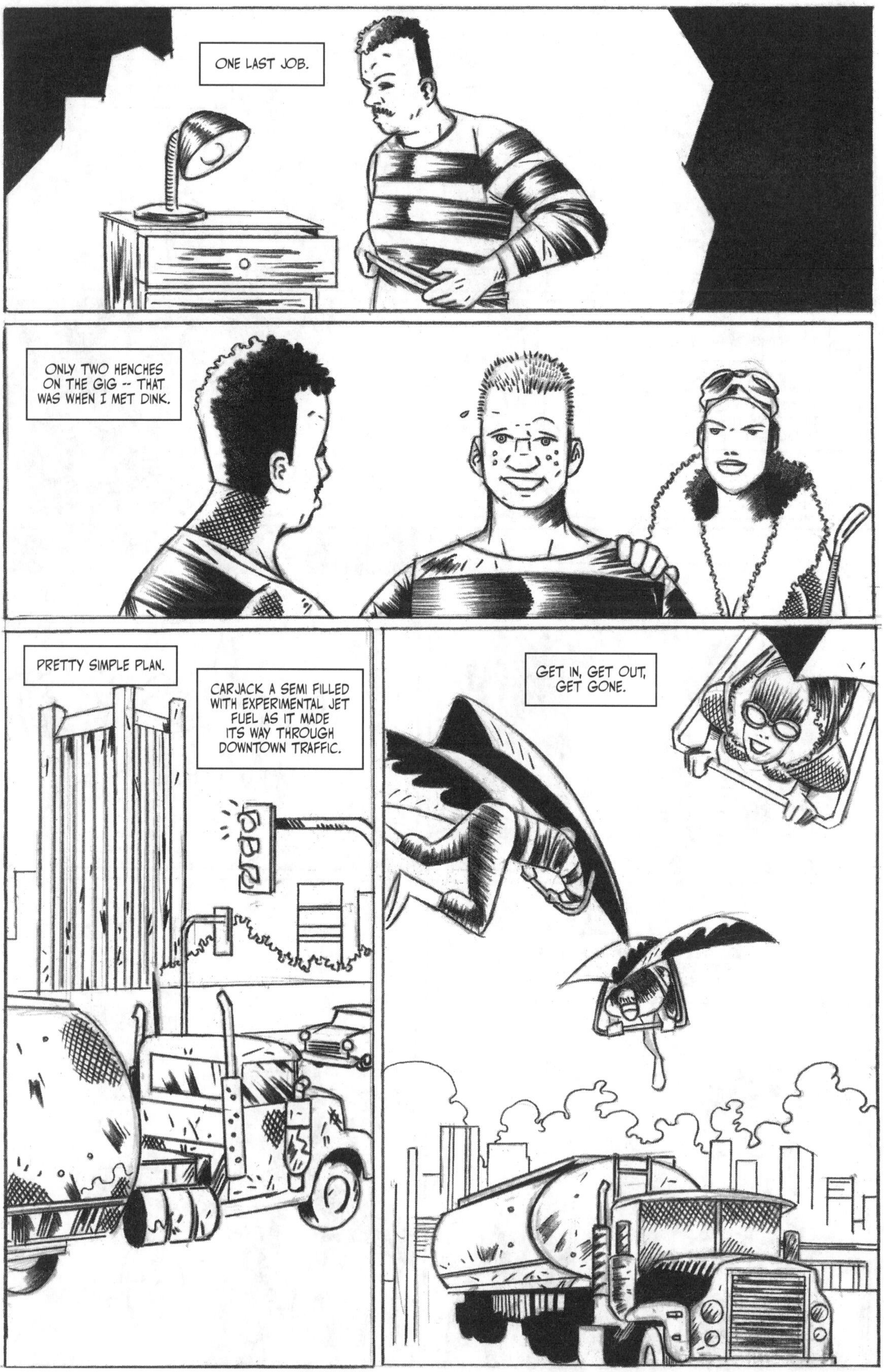

ONE LAST JOB.
ONLY TWO HENCHES ON THE GIG -- THAT WAS WHEN I MET DINK.
PRETTY SIMPLE PLAN.
CARJACK A SEMI FILLED WITH EXPERIMENTAL JET FUEL AS IT MADE ITS WAY THROUGH DOWNTOWN TRAFFIC.
GET IN, GET OUT, GET GONE.

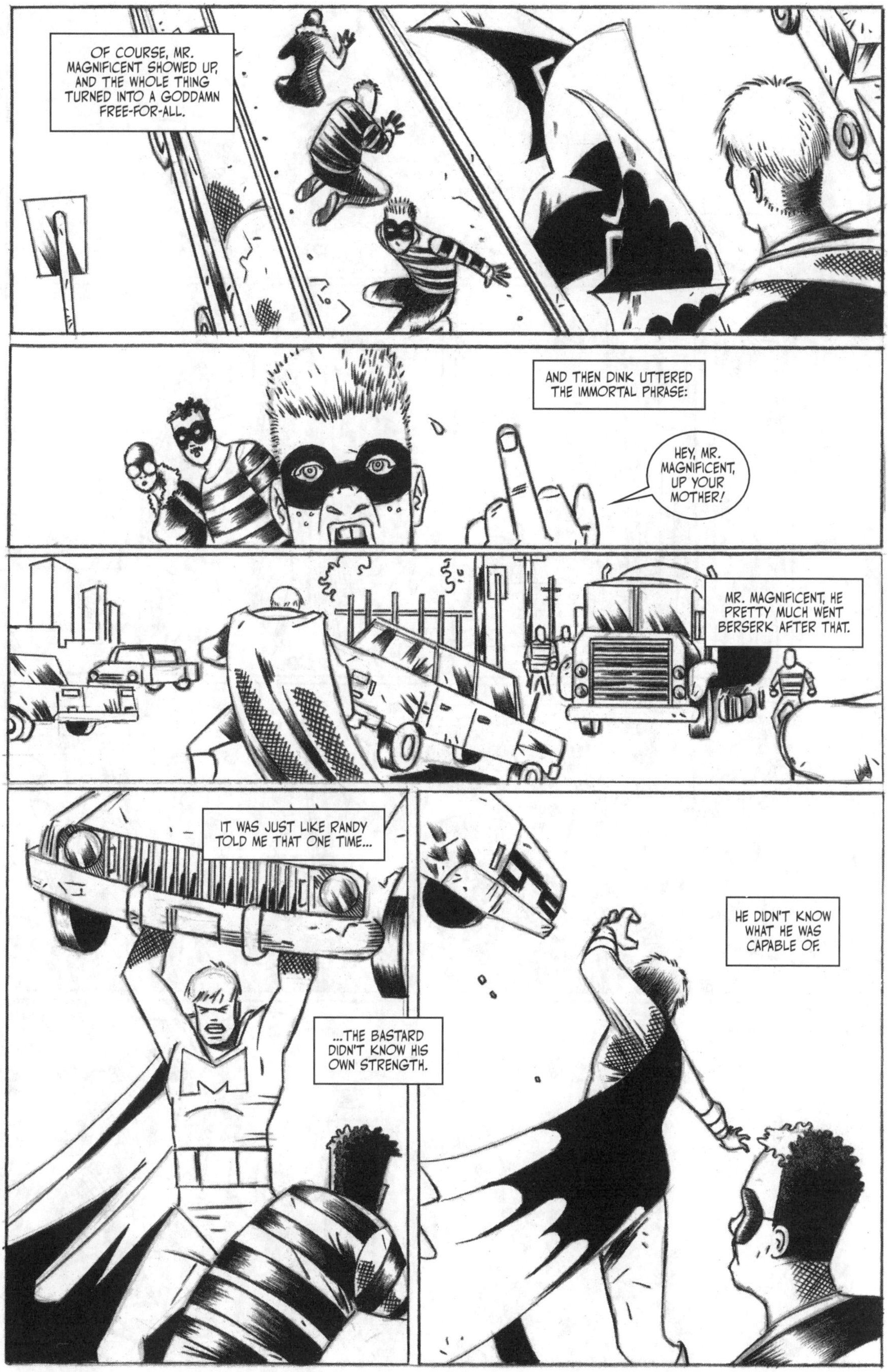
OF COURSE, MR. MAGNIFICENT SHOWED UP, AND THE WHOLE THING TURNED INTO A GODDAMN FREE-FOR-ALL.
AND THEN DINK UTTERED THE IMMORTAL PHRASE:
HEY, MR. MAGNIFICENT, UP YOUR MOTHER!
MR. MAGNIFICENT, HE PRETTY MUCH WENT BERSERK AFTER THAT.
IT WAS JUST LIKE RANDY TOLD ME THAT ONE TIME...
...THE BASTARD DIDN'T KNOW HIS OWN STRENGTH.
HE DIDN'T KNOW WHAT HE WAS CAPABLE OF.

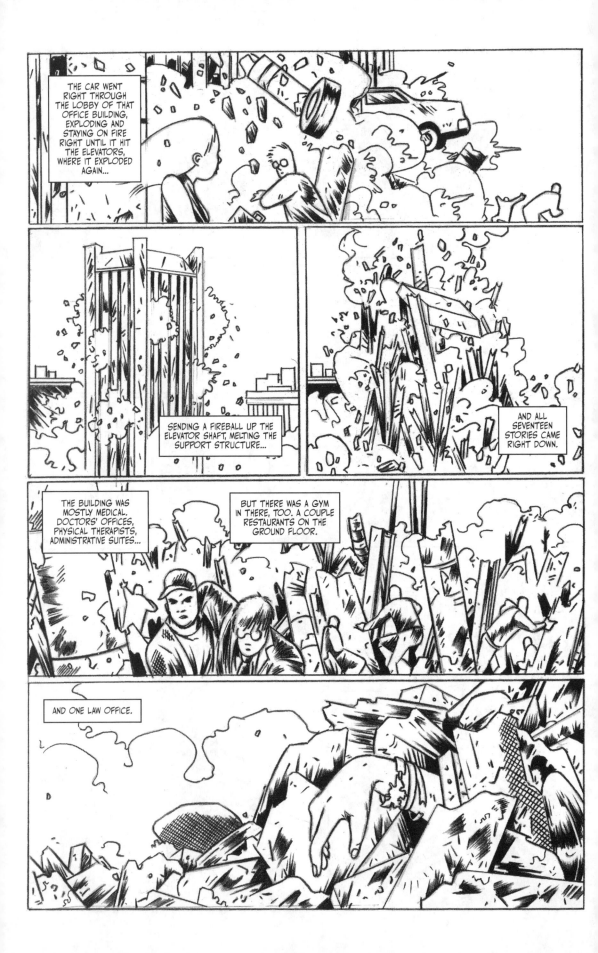

THE CAR WENT RIGHT THROUGH THE LOBBY OF THAT OFFICE BUILDING, EXPLODING AND STAYING ON FIRE RIGHT UNTIL IT HIT THE ELEVATORS, WHERE IT EXPLODED AGAIN...

SENDING A FIREBALL UP THE ELEVATOR SHAFT, MELTING THE SUPPORT STRUCTURE...

AND ALL SEVENTEEN STORIES CAME RIGHT DOWN.

THE BUILDING WAS MOSTLY MEDICAL. DOCTORS' OFFICES, PHYSICAL THERAPISTS, ADMINISTRATIVE SUITES...

BUT THERE WAS A GYM IN THERE, TOO. A COUPLE RESTAURANTS ON THE GROUND FLOOR.

AND ONE LAW OFFICE.

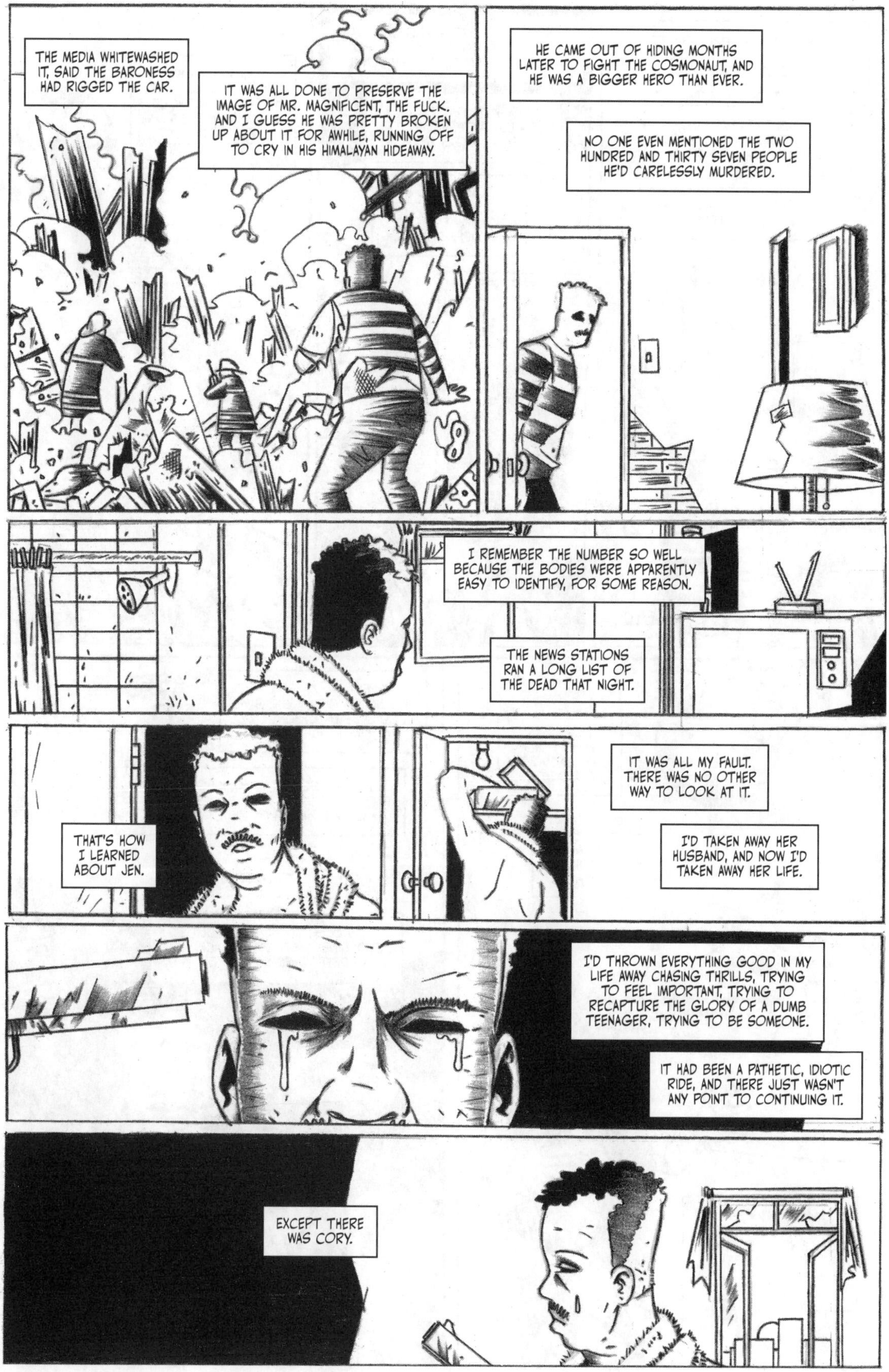
THE MEDIA WHITEWASHED IT, SAID THE BARONESS HAD RIGGED THE CAR.
IT WAS ALL DONE TO PRESERVE THE IMAGE OF MR. MAGNIFICENT, THE FUCK. AND I GUESS HE WAS PRETTY BROKEN UP ABOUT IT FOR AWHILE, RUNNING OFF TO CRY IN HIS HIMALAYAN HIDEAWAY.
HE CAME OUT OF HIDING MONTHS LATER TO FIGHT THE COSMONAUT, AND HE WAS A BIGGER HERO THAN EVER.
NO ONE EVEN MENTIONED THE TWO HUNDRED AND THIRTY SEVEN PEOPLE HE'D CARELESSLY MURDERED.
I REMEMBER THE NUMBER SO WELL BECAUSE THE BODIES WERE APPARENTLY EASY TO IDENTIFY, FOR SOME REASON.
THE NEWS STATIONS RAN A LONG LIST OF THE DEAD THAT NIGHT.
THAT'S HOW I LEARNED ABOUT JEN.
IT WAS ALL MY FAULT. THERE WAS NO OTHER WAY TO LOOK AT IT.
I'D TAKEN AWAY HER HUSBAND, AND NOW I'D TAKEN AWAY HER LIFE.
I'D THROWN EVERYTHING GOOD IN MY LIFE AWAY CHASING THRILLS, TRYING TO FEEL IMPORTANT, TRYING TO RECAPTURE THE GLORY OF A DUMB TEENAGER, TRYING TO BE SOMEONE.
IT HAD BEEN A PATHETIC, IDIOTIC RIDE, AND THERE JUST WASN'T ANY POINT TO CONTINUING IT.
EXCEPT THERE WAS CORY.

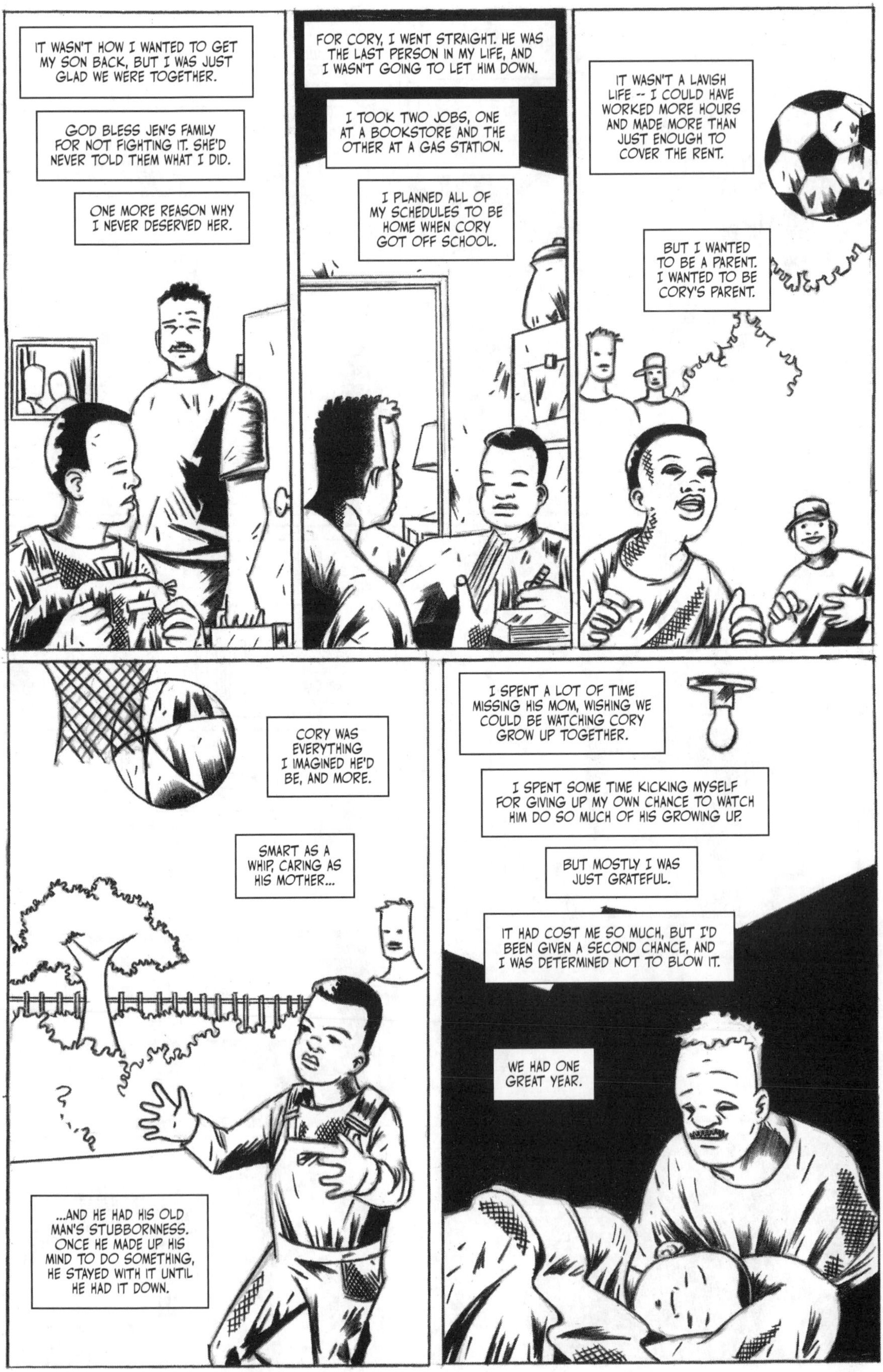
IT WASN'T HOW I WANTED TO GET MY SON BACK, BUT I WAS JUST GLAD WE WERE TOGETHER.
GOD BLESS JEN'S FAMILY FOR NOT FIGHTING IT. SHE'D NEVER TOLD THEM WHAT I DID.
ONE MORE REASON WHY I NEVER DESERVED HER.
FOR CORY, I WENT STRAIGHT. HE WAS THE LAST PERSON IN MY LIFE, AND I WASN'T GOING TO LET HIM DOWN.
I TOOK TWO JOBS, ONE AT A BOOKSTORE AND THE OTHER AT A GAS STATION.
I PLANNED ALL OF MY SCHEDULES TO BE HOME WHEN CORY GOT OFF SCHOOL.
IT WASN'T A LAVISH LIFE -- I COULD HAVE WORKED MORE HOURS AND MADE MORE THAN JUST ENOUGH TO COVER THE RENT.
BUT I WANTED TO BE A PARENT. I WANTED TO BE CORY'S PARENT.
CORY WAS EVERYTHING I IMAGINED HE'D BE, AND MORE.
SMART AS A WHIP, CARING AS HIS MOTHER...
...AND HE HAD HIS OLD MAN'S STUBBORNNESS. ONCE HE MADE UP HIS MIND TO DO SOMETHING, HE STAYED WITH IT UNTIL HE HAD IT DOWN.
I SPENT A LOT OF TIME MISSING HIS MOM, WISHING WE COULD BE WATCHING CORY GROW UP TOGETHER.
I SPENT SOME TIME KICKING MYSELF FOR GIVING UP MY OWN CHANCE TO WATCH HIM DO SO MUCH OF HIS GROWING UP.
BUT MOSTLY I WAS JUST GRATEFUL.
IT HAD COST ME SO MUCH, BUT I'D BEEN GIVEN A SECOND CHANCE, AND I WAS DETERMINED NOT TO BLOW IT.
WE HAD ONE GREAT YEAR.

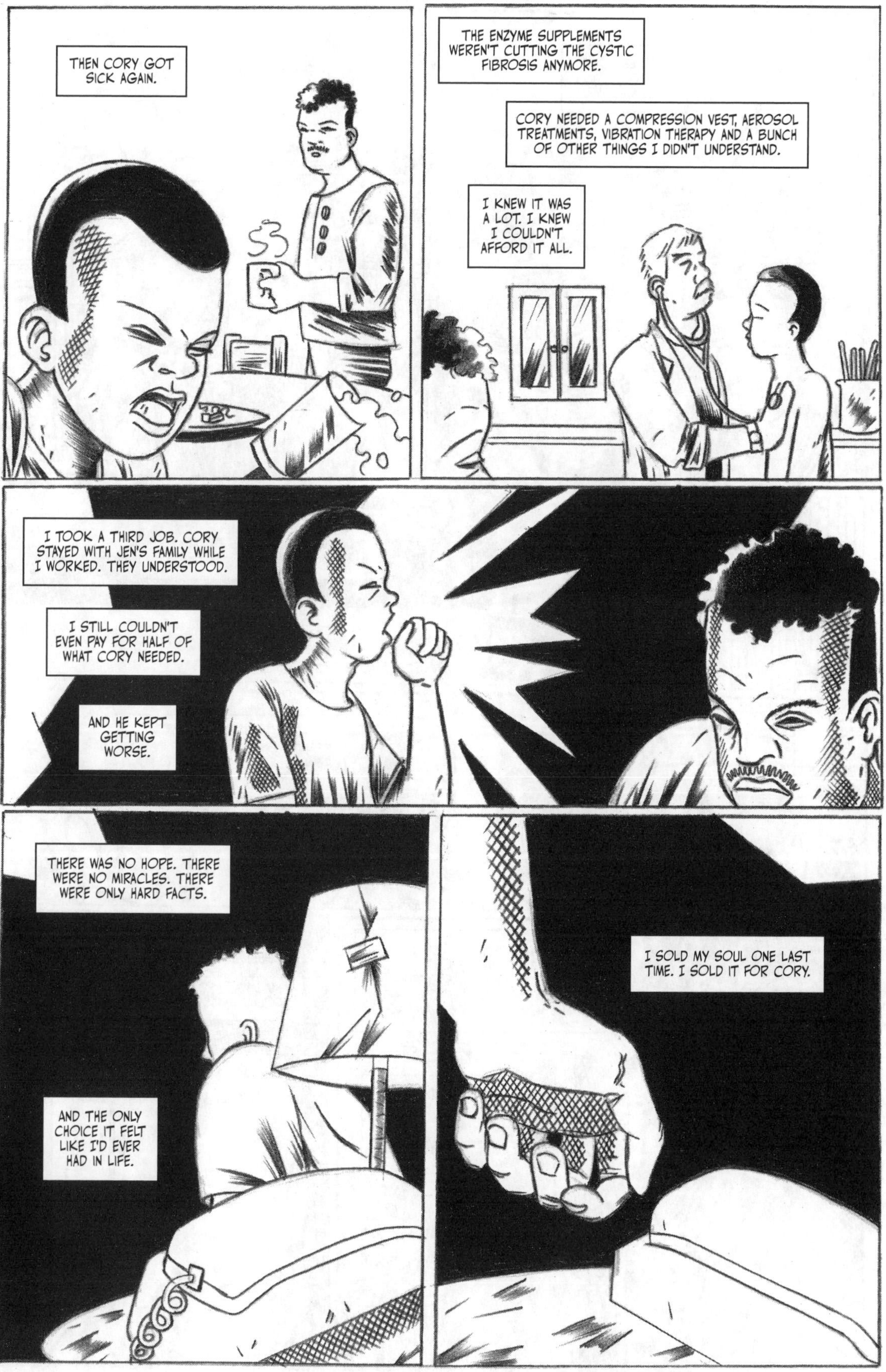
THEN CORY GOT SICK AGAIN.
THE ENZYME SUPPLEMENTS WEREN'T CUTTING THE CYSTIC FIBROSIS ANYMORE.
CORY NEEDED A COMPRESSION VEST, AEROSOL TREATMENTS, VIBRATION THERAPY AND A BUNCH OF OTHER THINGS I DIDN'T UNDERSTAND.
I KNEW IT WAS A LOT. I KNEW I COULDN'T AFFORD IT ALL.
I TOOK A THIRD JOB. CORY STAYED WITH JEN'S FAMILY WHILE I WORKED. THEY UNDERSTOOD.
I STILL COULDN'T EVEN PAY FOR HALF OF WHAT CORY NEEDED.
AND HE KEPT GETTING WORSE.
THERE WAS NO HOPE. THERE WERE NO MIRACLES. THERE WERE ONLY HARD FACTS.
AND THE ONLY CHOICE IT FELT LIKE I'D EVER HAD IN LIFE.
I SOLD MY SOUL ONE LAST TIME. I SOLD IT FOR CORY.

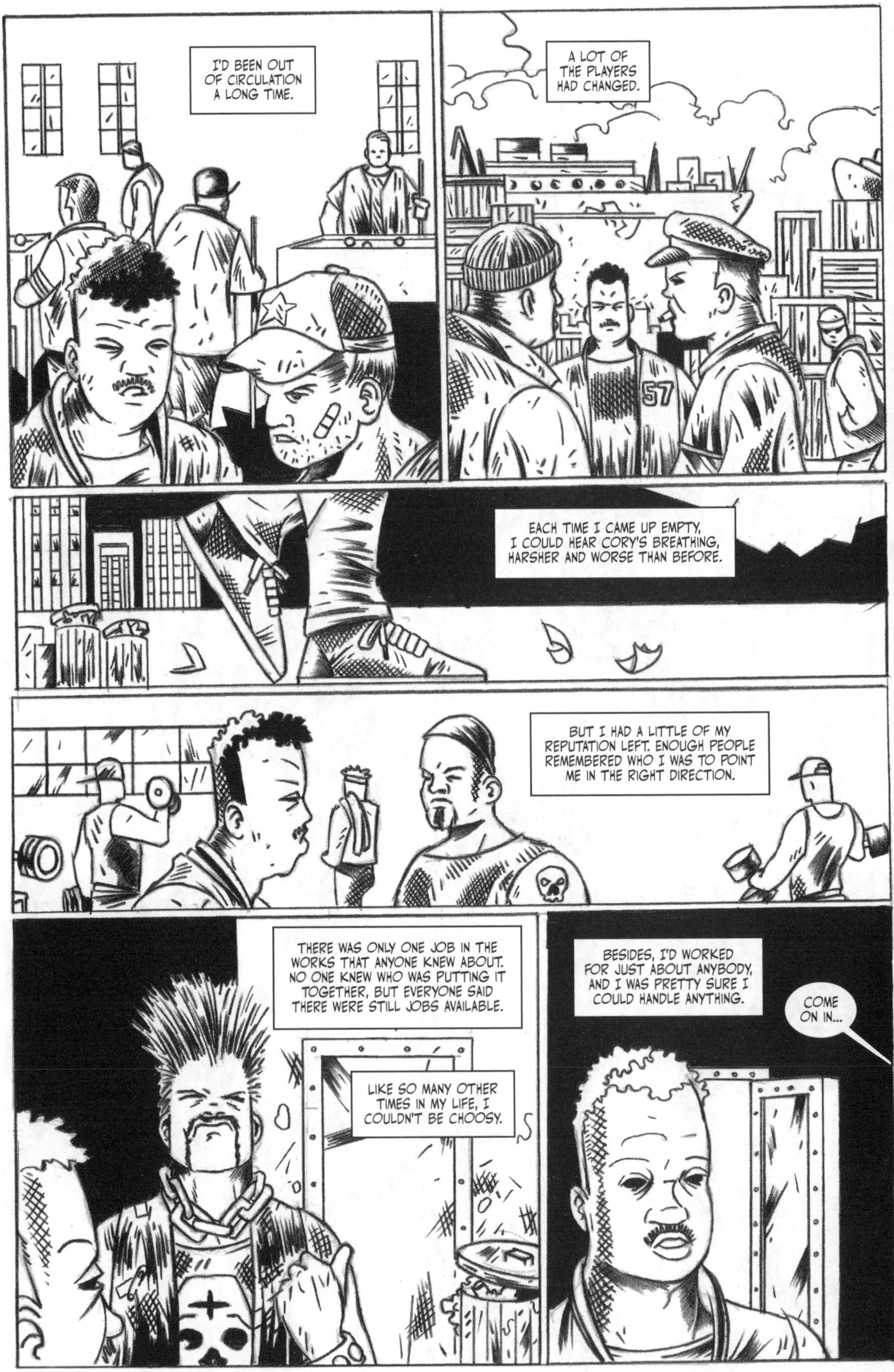

I'D BEEN OUT OF CIRCULATION A LONG TIME.
A LOT OF THE PLAYERS HAD CHANGED.
57
EACH TIME I CAME UP EMPTY, I COULD HEAR CORY'S BREATHING, HARSHER AND WORSE THAN BEFORE.
BUT I HAD A LITTLE OF MY REPUTATION LEFT. ENOUGH PEOPLE REMEMBERED WHO I WAS TO POINT ME IN THE RIGHT DIRECTION.
THERE WAS ONLY ONE JOB IN THE WORKS THAT ANYONE KNEW ABOUT. NO ONE KNEW WHO WAS PUTTING IT TOGETHER, BUT EVERYONE SAID THERE WERE STILL JOBS AVAILABLE.
LIKE SO MANY OTHER TIMES IN MY LIFE, I COULDN'T BE CHOOSY.
BESIDES, I'D WORKED FOR JUST ABOUT ANYBODY, AND I WAS PRETTY SURE I COULD HANDLE ANYTHING.
COME ON IN...

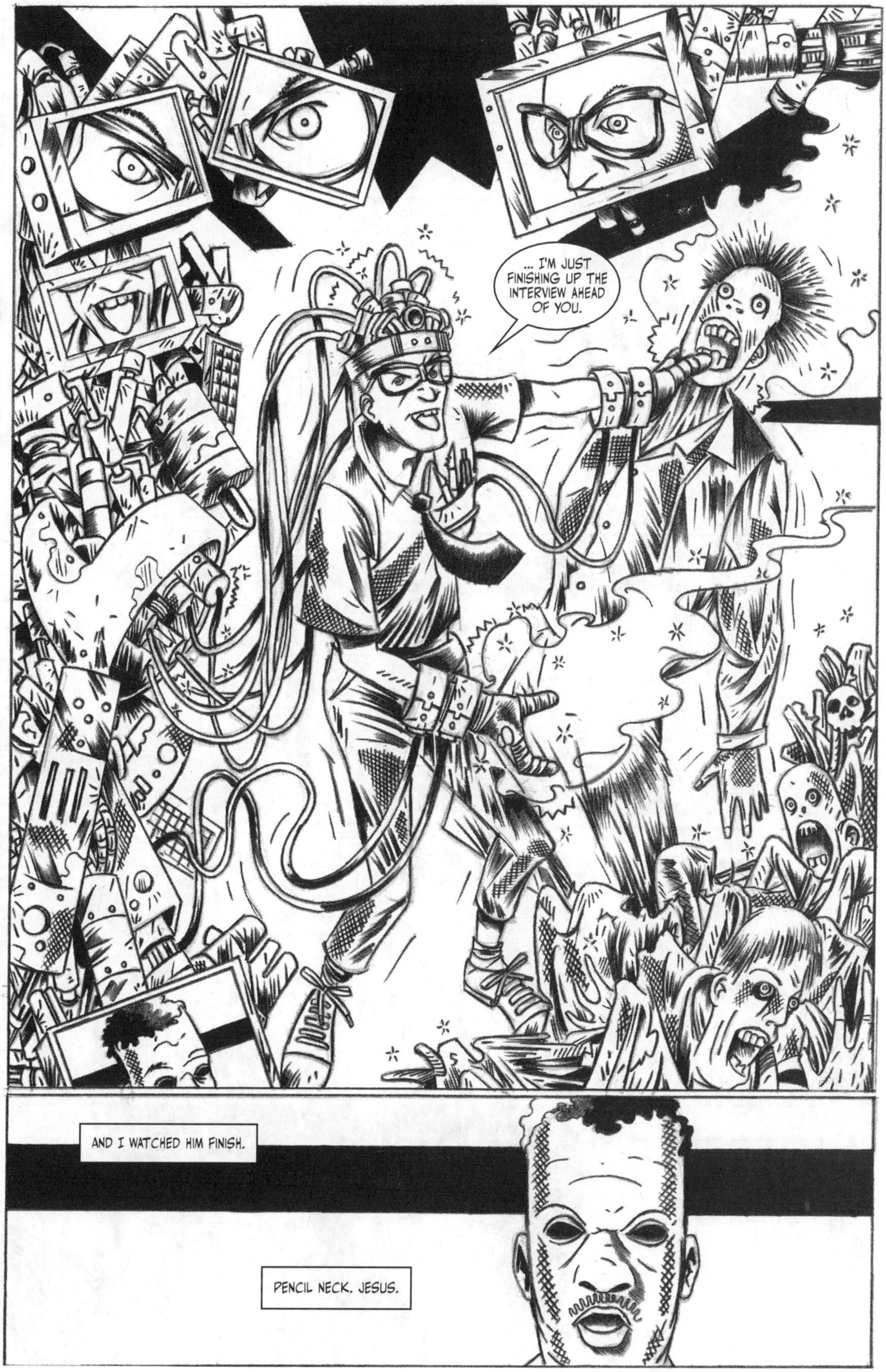
... I'M JUST FINISHING UP THE INTERVIEW AHEAD OF YOU.
AND I WATCHED HIM FINISH.
PENCIL NECK. JESUS.

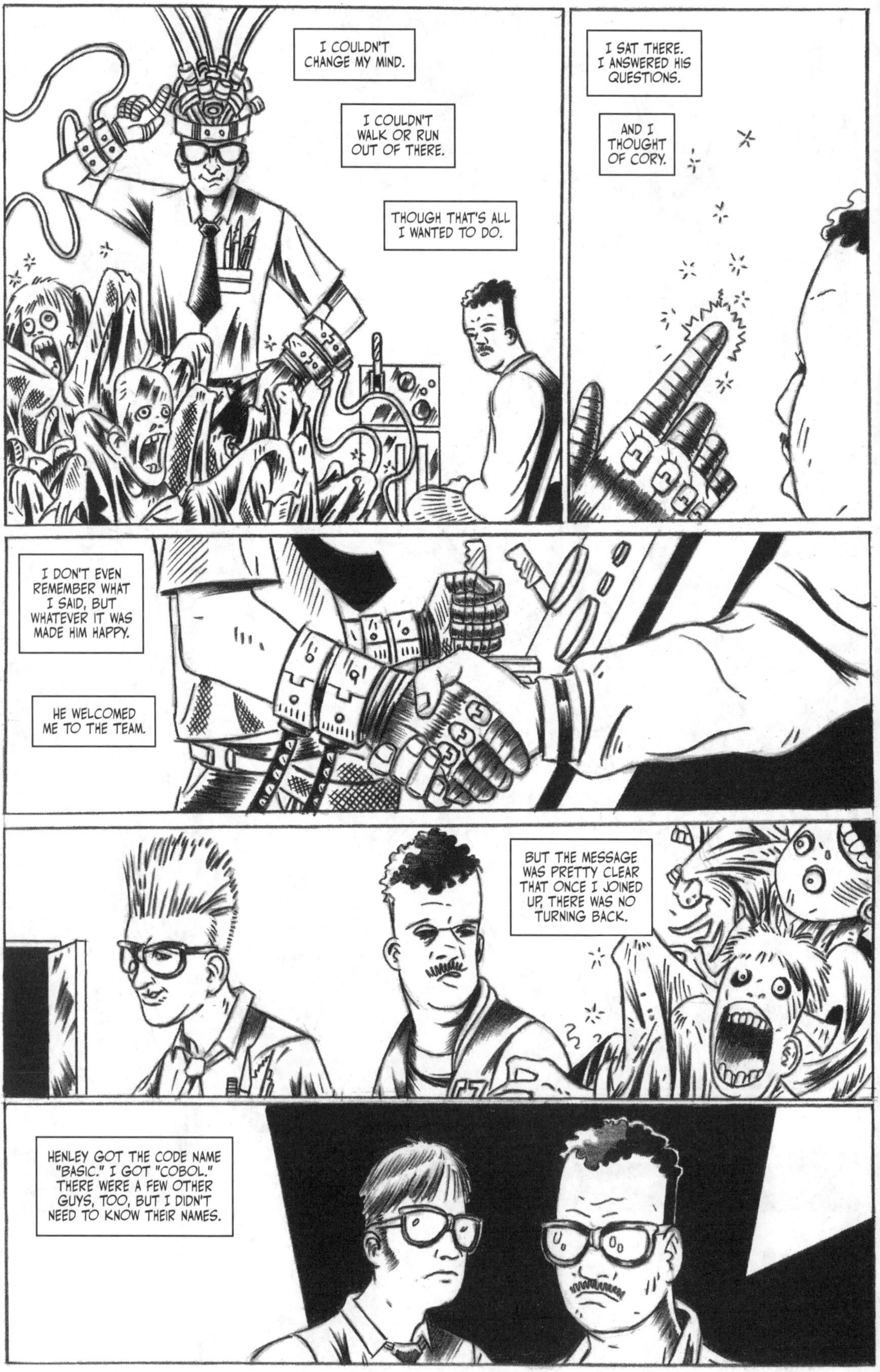
I COULDN'T CHANGE MY MIND.
I COULDN'T WALK OR RUN OUT OF THERE.
THOUGH THAT'S ALL I WANTED TO DO.
I SAT THERE. I ANSWERED HIS QUESTIONS.
AND I THOUGHT OF CORY.
I DON'T EVEN REMEMBER WHAT I SAID, BUT WHATEVER IT WAS MADE HIM HAPPY.
HE WELCOMED ME TO THE TEAM.
BUT THE MESSAGE WAS PRETTY CLEAR THAT ONCE I JOINED UP, THERE WAS NO TURNING BACK.
HENLEY GOT THE CODE NAME "BASIC." I GOT "COBOL." THERE WERE A FEW OTHER GUYS, TOO, BUT I DIDN'T NEED TO KNOW THEIR NAMES.

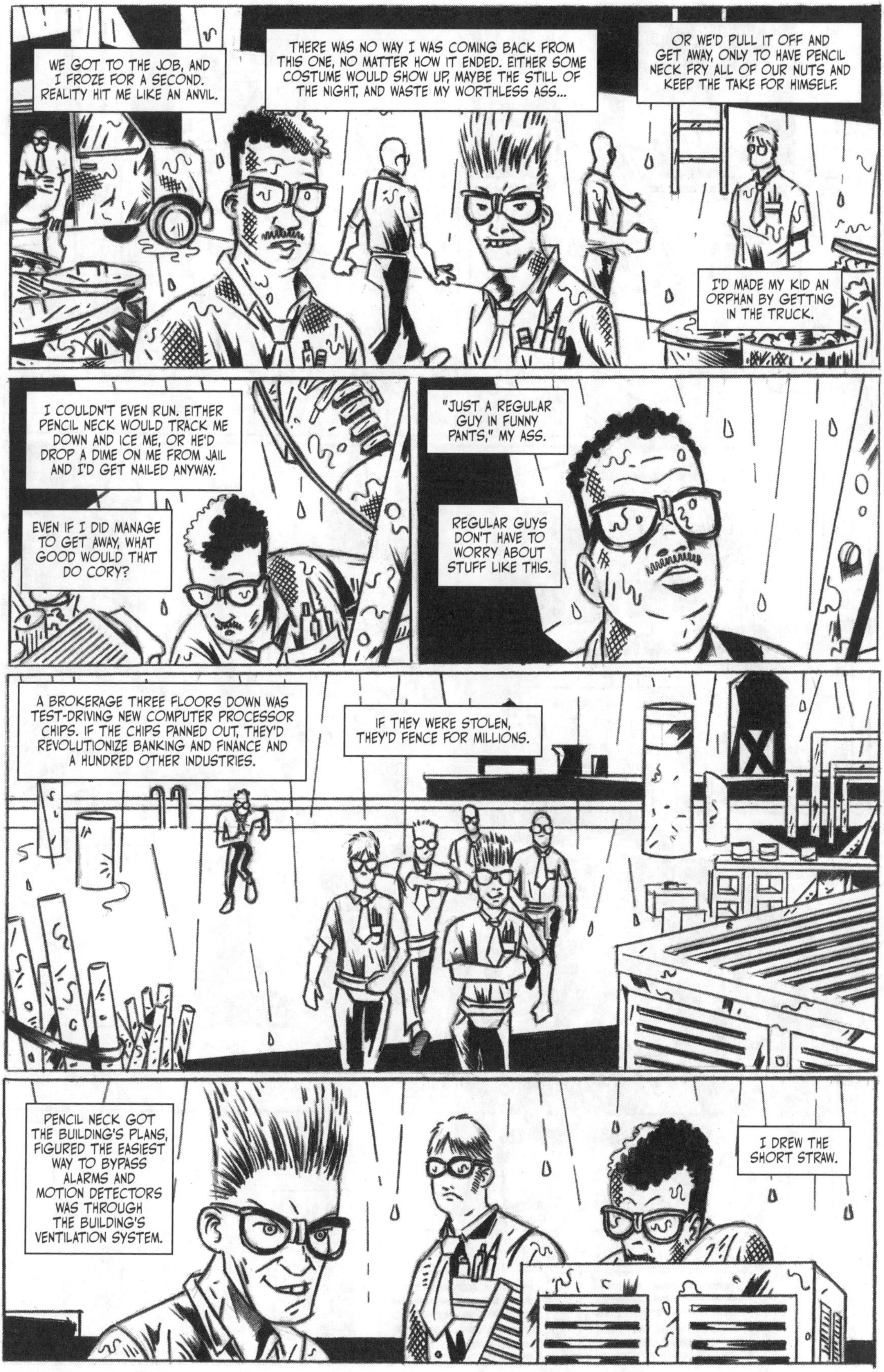
WE GOT TO THE JOB, AND I FROZE FOR A SECOND. REALITY HIT ME LIKE AN ANVIL.
THERE WAS NO WAY I WAS COMING BACK FROM THIS ONE, NO MATTER HOW IT ENDED. EITHER SOME COSTUME WOULD SHOW UP, MAYBE THE STILL OF THE NIGHT, AND WASTE MY WORTHLESS ASS...
OR WE'D PULL IT OFF AND GET AWAY, ONLY TO HAVE PENCIL NECK FRY ALL OF OUR NUTS AND KEEP THE TAKE FOR HIMSELF.
I'D MADE MY KID AN ORPHAN BY GETTING IN THE TRUCK.
I COULDN'T EVEN RUN. EITHER PENCIL NECK WOULD TRACK ME DOWN AND ICE ME, OR HE'D DROP A DIME ON ME FROM JAIL AND I'D GET NAILED ANYWAY.
EVEN IF I DID MANAGE TO GET AWAY, WHAT GOOD WOULD THAT DO CORY?
"JUST A REGULAR GUY IN FUNNY PANTS," MY ASS.
REGULAR GUYS DON'T HAVE TO WORRY ABOUT STUFF LIKE THIS.
A BROKERAGE THREE FLOORS DOWN WAS TEST-DRIVING NEW COMPUTER PROCESSOR CHIPS. IF THE CHIPS PANNED OUT, THEY'D REVOLUTIONIZE BANKING AND FINANCE AND A HUNDRED OTHER INDUSTRIES.
IF THEY WERE STOLEN, THEY'D FENCE FOR MILLIONS.
PENCIL NECK GOT THE BUILDING'S PLANS, FIGURED THE EASIEST WAY TO BYPASS ALARMS AND MOTION DETECTORS WAS THROUGH THE BUILDING'S VENTILATION SYSTEM.
I DREW THE SHORT STRAW.

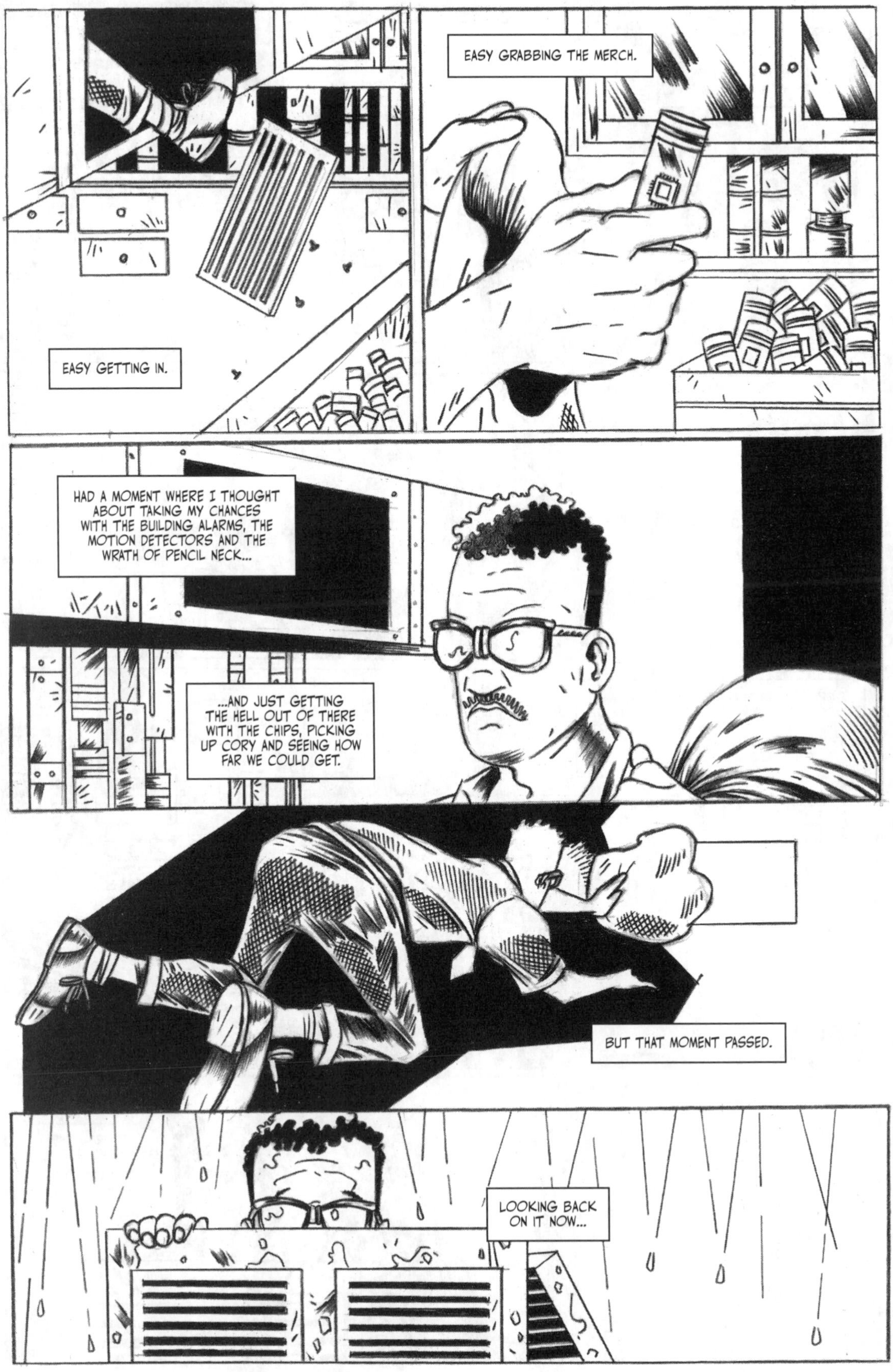
EASY GETTING IN.
EASY GRABBING THE MERCH.
HAD A MOMENT WHERE I THOUGHT ABOUT TAKING MY CHANCES WITH THE BUILDING ALARMS, THE MOTION DETECTORS AND THE WRATH OF PENCIL NECK...
...AND JUST GETTING THE HELL OUT OF THERE WITH THE CHIPS, PICKING UP CORY AND SEEING HOW FAR WE COULD GET.
BUT THAT MOMENT PASSED.
LOOKING BACK ON IT NOW...

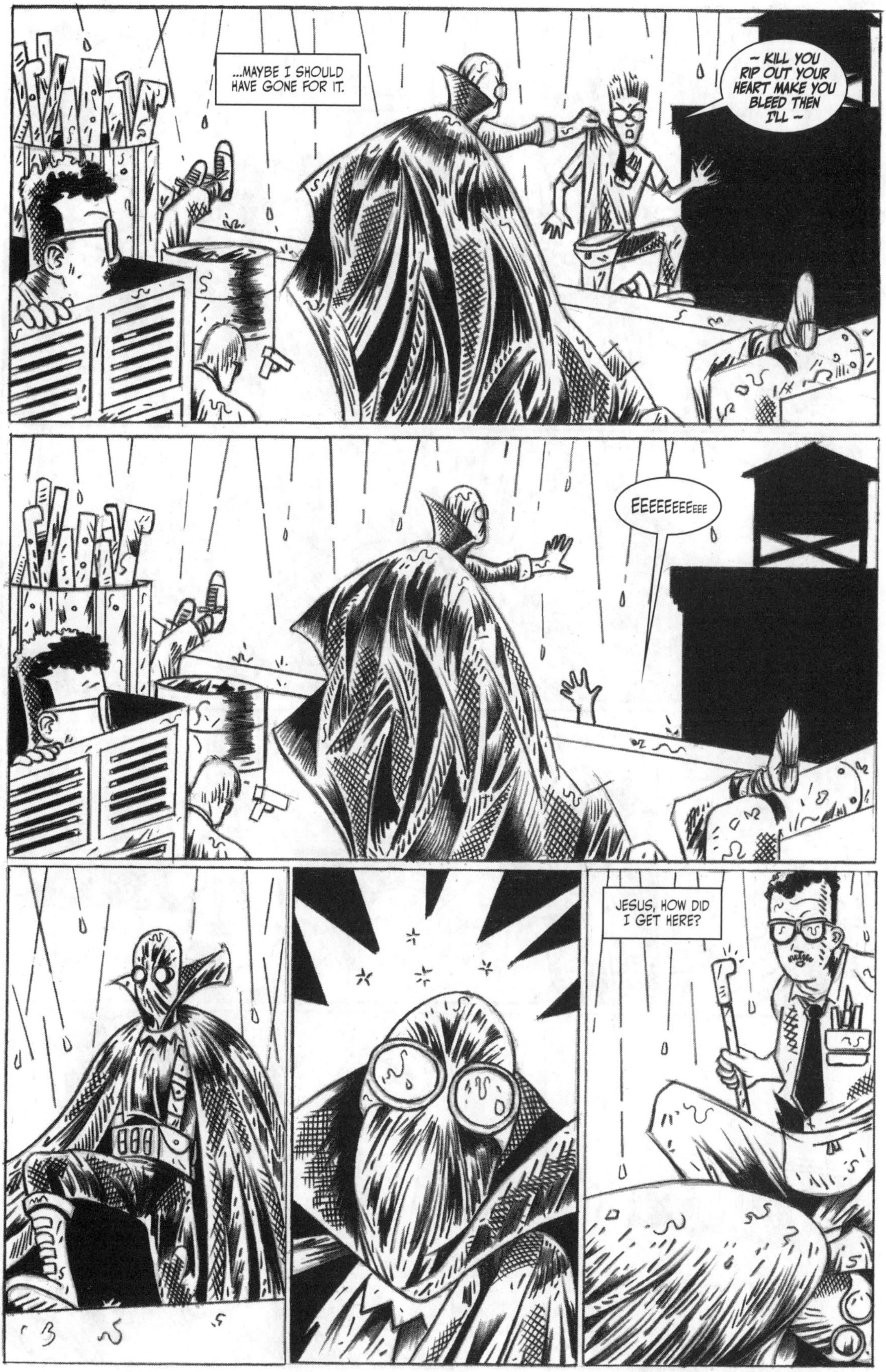
...MAYBE I SHOULD HAVE GONE FOR IT.
~ KILL YOU RIP OUT YOUR HEART MAKE YOU BLEED THEN I'LL ~
EEEEEEEEeee
JESUS, HOW DID I GET HERE?

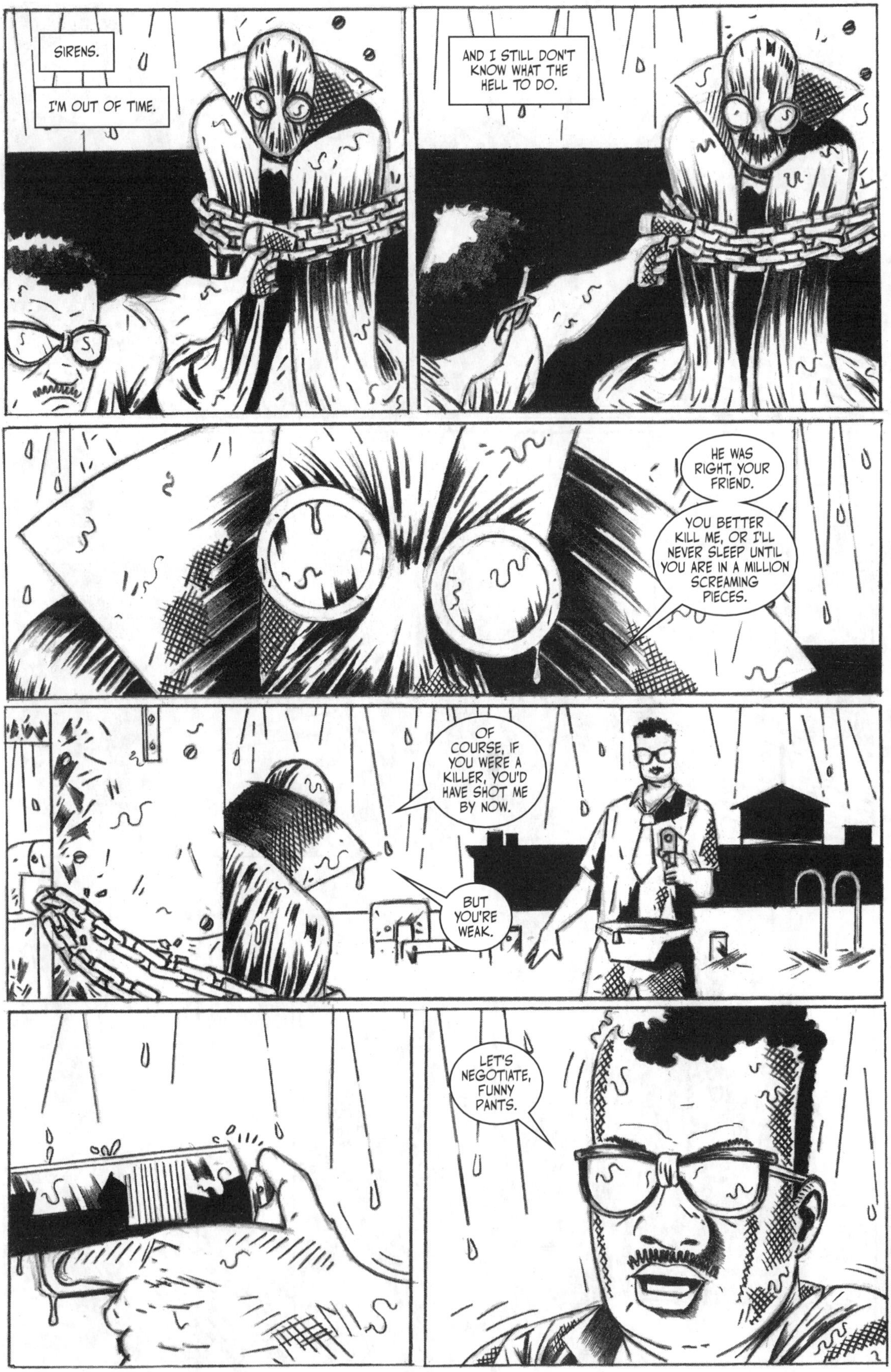
SIRENS.
I'M OUT OF TIME.
AND I STILL DON'T KNOW WHAT THE HELL TO DO.
HE WAS RIGHT, YOUR FRIEND.
YOU BETTER KILL ME, OR I'LL NEVER SLEEP UNTIL YOU ARE IN A MILLION SCREAMING PIECES.
OF COURSE, IF YOU WERE A KILLER, YOU'D HAVE SHOT ME BY NOW.
BUT YOU'RE WEAK.
LET'S NEGOTIATE, FUNNY PANTS.

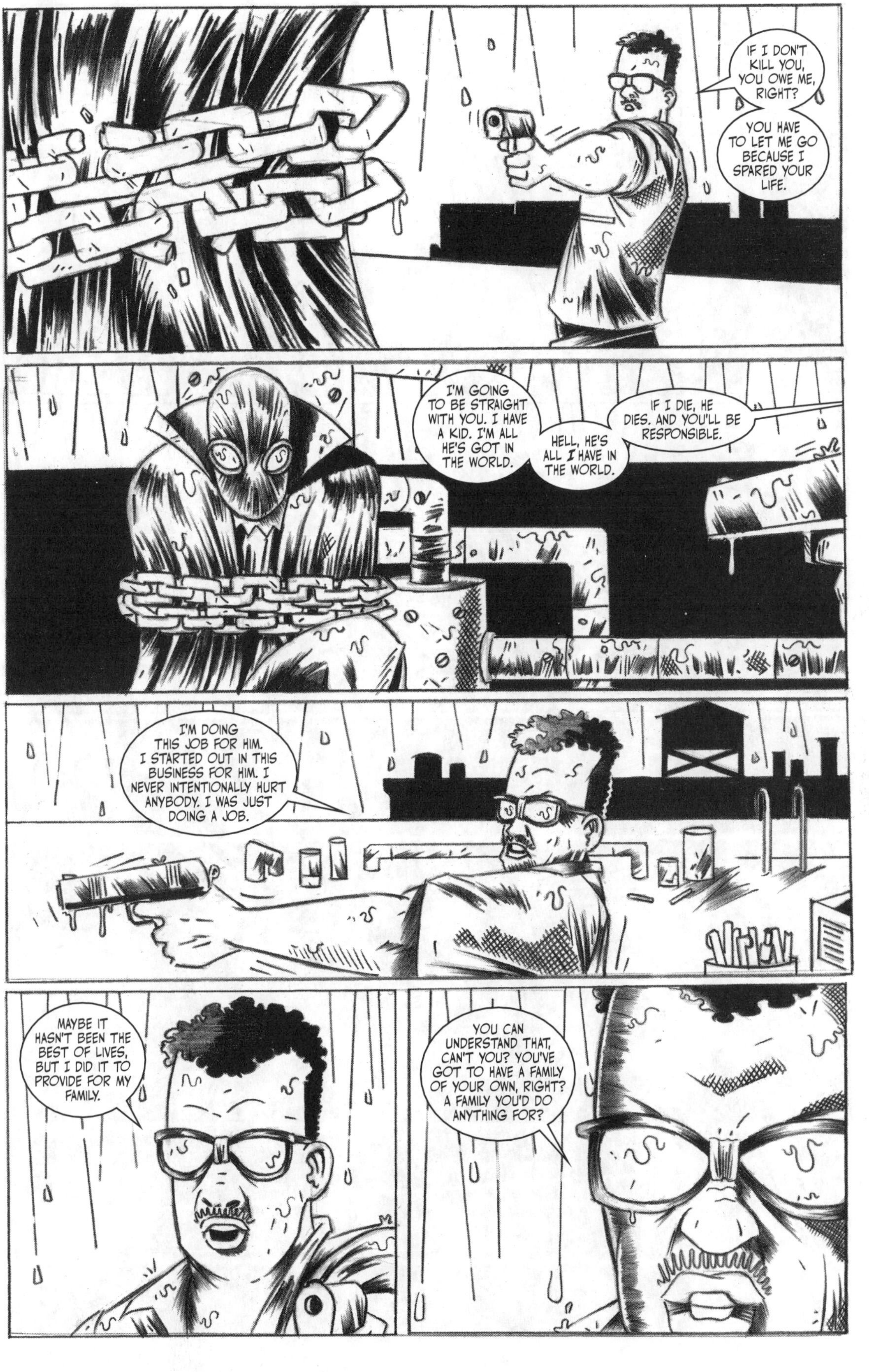
IF I DON'T KILL YOU, YOU OWE ME, RIGHT?
YOU HAVE TO LET ME GO BECAUSE I SPARED YOUR LIFE.
I'M GOING TO BE STRAIGHT WITH YOU. I HAVE A KID. I'M ALL HE'S GOT IN THE WORLD.
HELL, HE'S ALL I HAVE IN THE WORLD.
IF I DIE, HE DIES. AND YOU'LL BE RESPONSIBLE.
I'M DOING THIS JOB FOR HIM. I STARTED OUT IN THIS BUSINESS FOR HIM. I NEVER INTENTIONALLY HURT ANYBODY. I WAS JUST DOING A JOB.
MAYBE IT HASN'T BEEN THE BEST OF LIVES, BUT I DID IT TO PROVIDE FOR MY FAMILY.
YOU CAN UNDERSTAND THAT, CAN'T YOU? YOU'VE GOT TO HAVE A FAMILY OF YOUR OWN, RIGHT? A FAMILY YOU'D DO ANYTHING FOR?

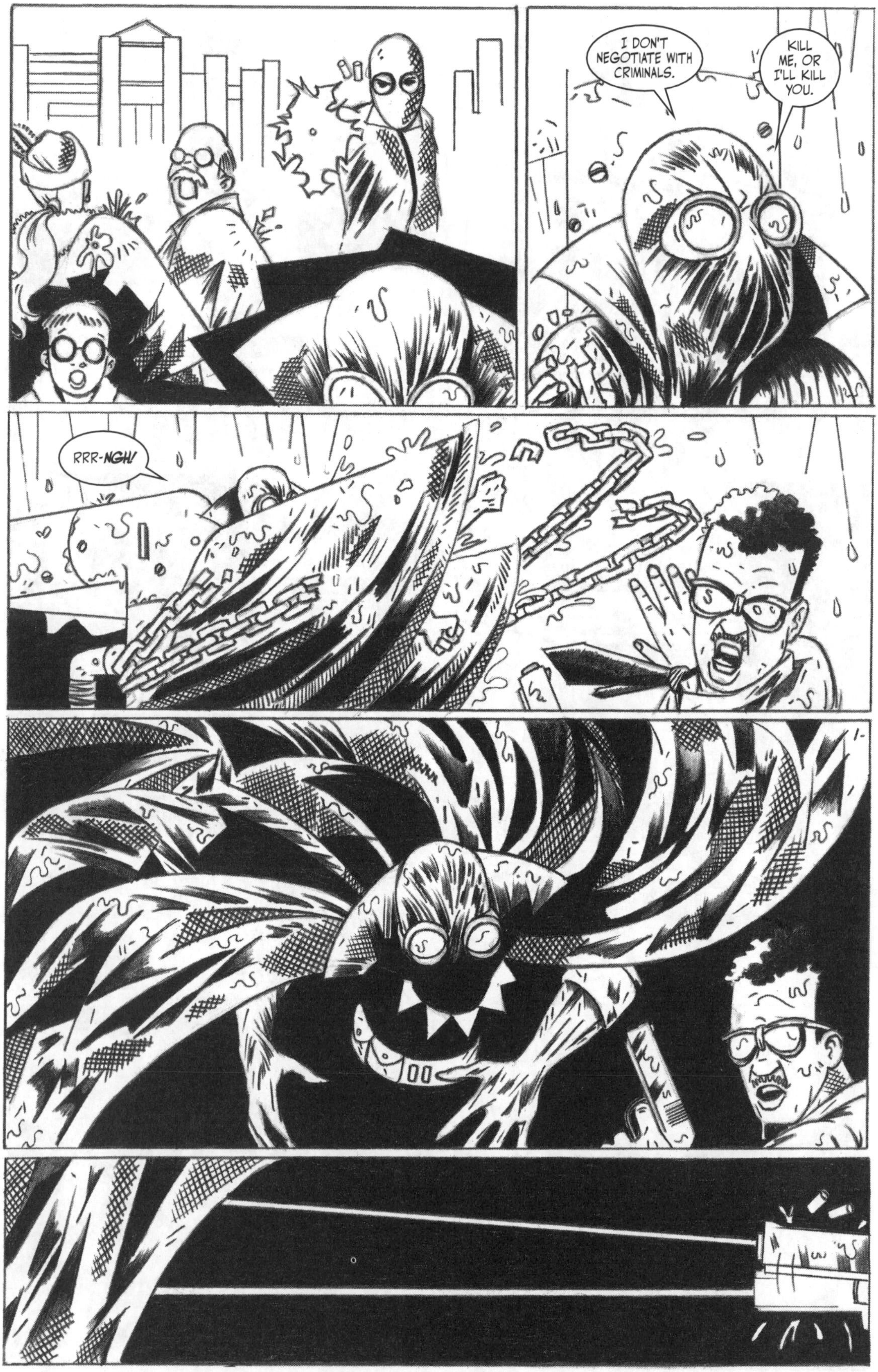
I DON'T NEGOTIATE WITH CRIMINALS.
KILL ME, OR I'LL KILL YOU.
RRR-NGH!

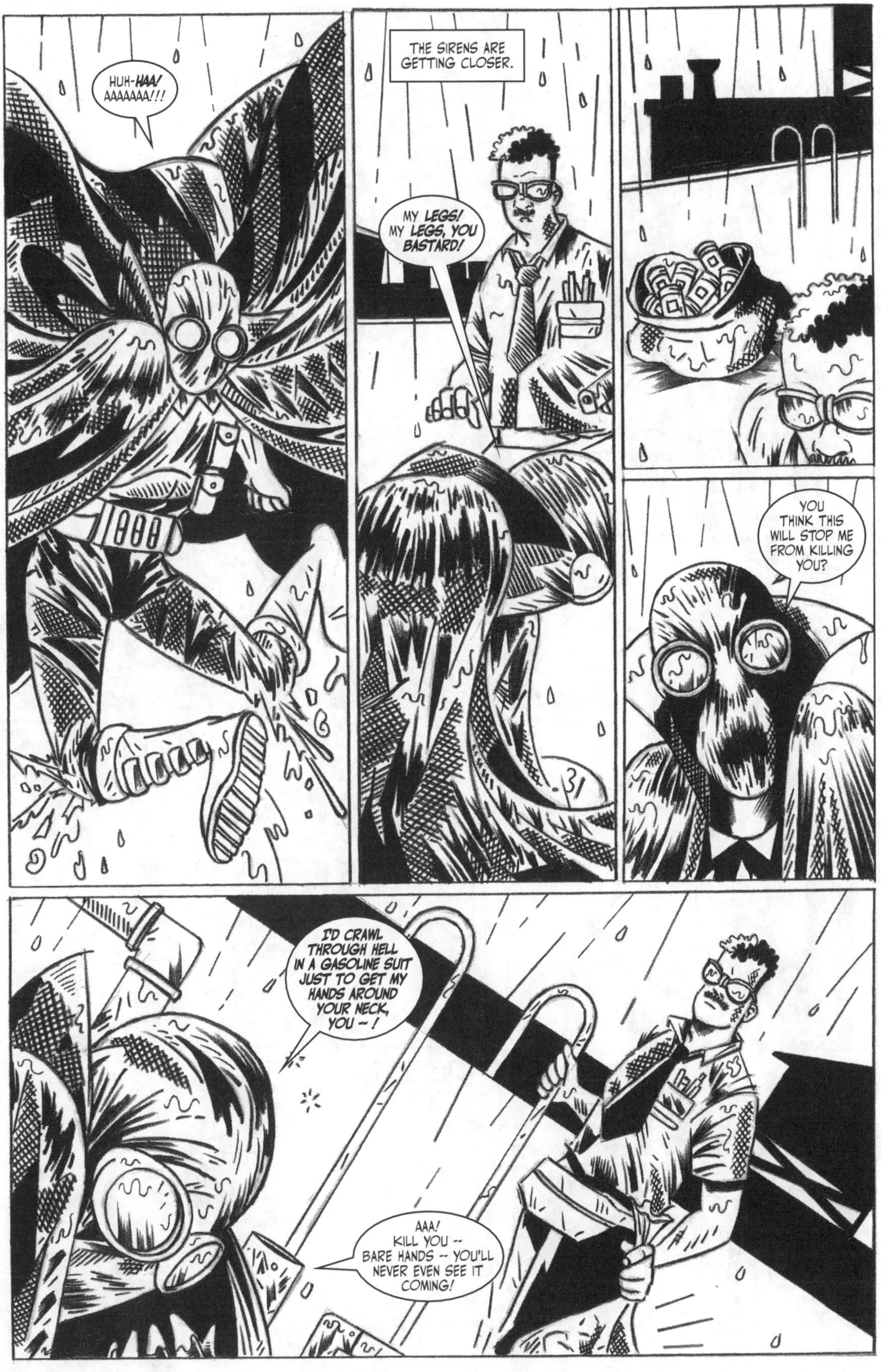
HUH-HAA! AAAAAAA!!!
THE SIRENS ARE GETTING CLOSER.
MY LEGS! MY LEGS, YOU BASTARD!
YOU THINK THIS WILL STOP ME FROM KILLING YOU?
I'D CRAWL THROUGH HELL IN A GASOLINE SUIT JUST TO GET MY HANDS AROUND YOUR NECK, YOU -- !
AAA! KILL YOU -- BARE HANDS -- YOU'LL NEVER EVEN SEE IT COMING!

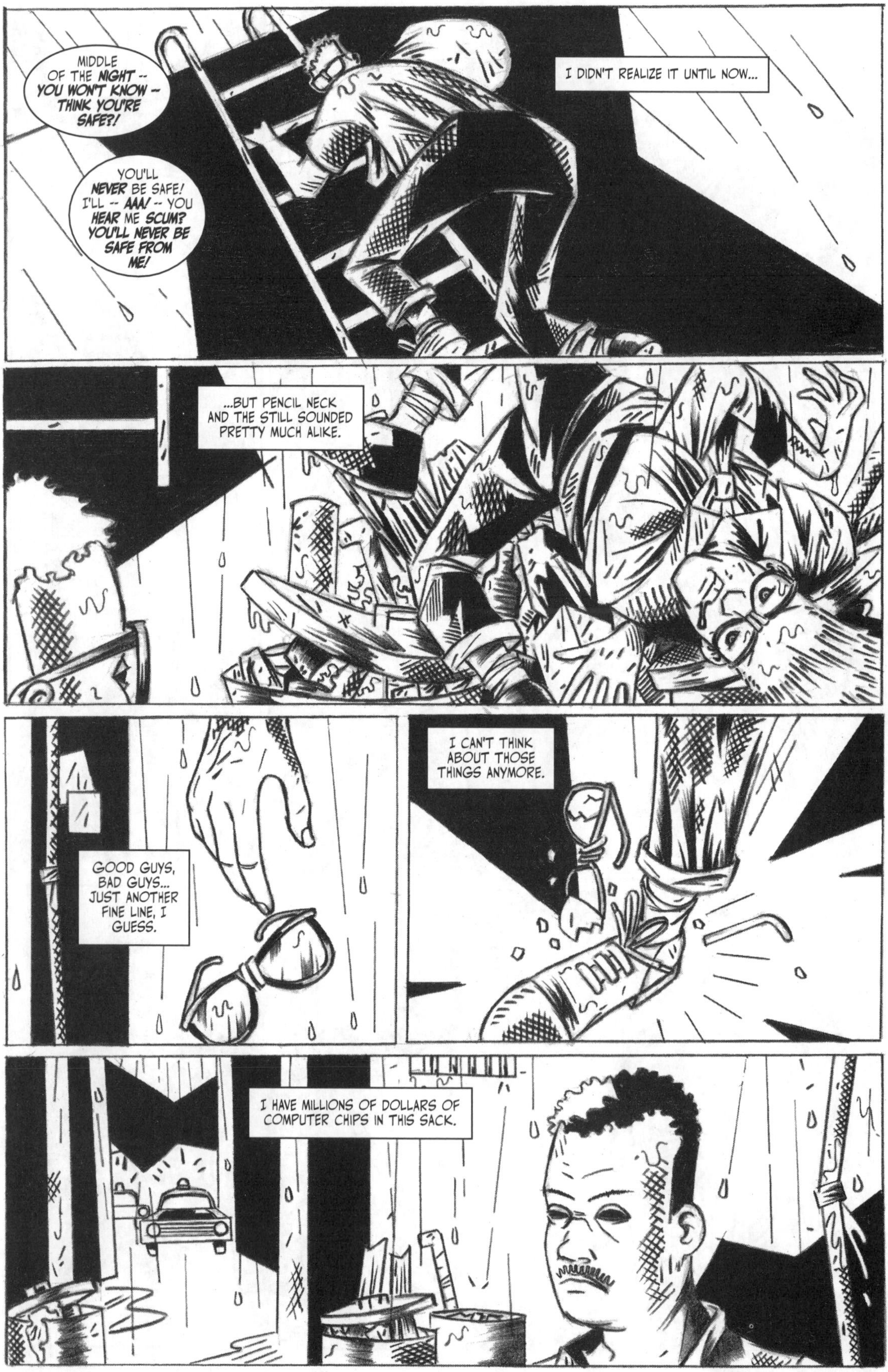
MIDDLE OF THE NIGHT -- YOU WON'T KNOW -- THINK YOU'RE SAFE?!
YOU'LL NEVER BE SAFE! I'LL -- AAA! -- YOU HEAR ME SCUM? YOU'LL NEVER BE SAFE FROM ME!
I DIDN'T REALIZE IT UNTIL NOW...
...BUT PENCIL NECK AND THE STILL SOUNDED PRETTY MUCH ALIKE.
GOOD GUYS, BAD GUYS... JUST ANOTHER FINE LINE, I GUESS.
I CAN'T THINK ABOUT THOSE THINGS ANYMORE.
I HAVE MILLIONS OF DOLLARS OF COMPUTER CHIPS IN THIS SACK.

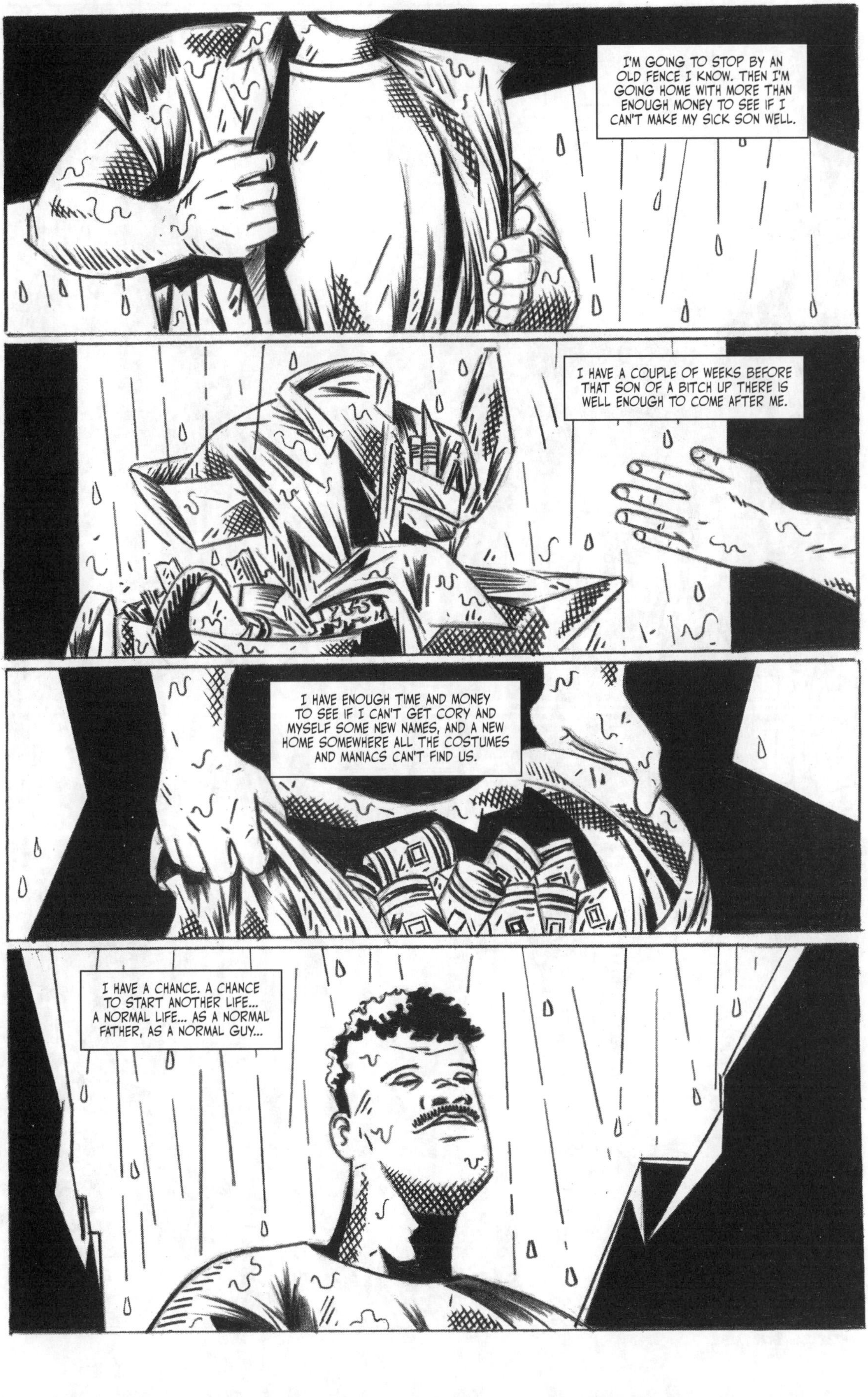
I'M GOING TO STOP BY AN OLD FENCE I KNOW. THEN I'M GOING HOME WITH MORE THAN ENOUGH MONEY TO SEE IF I CAN'T MAKE MY SICK SON WELL.
I HAVE A COUPLE OF WEEKS BEFORE THAT SON OF A BITCH UP THERE IS WELL ENOUGH TO COME AFTER ME.
I HAVE ENOUGH TIME AND MONEY TO SEE IF I CAN'T GET CORY AND MYSELF SOME NEW NAMES, AND A NEW HOME SOMEWHERE ALL THE COSTUMES AND MANIACS CAN'T FIND US.
I HAVE A CHANCE. A CHANCE TO START ANOTHER LIFE... A NORMAL LIFE... AS A NORMAL FATHER, AS A NORMAL GUY...

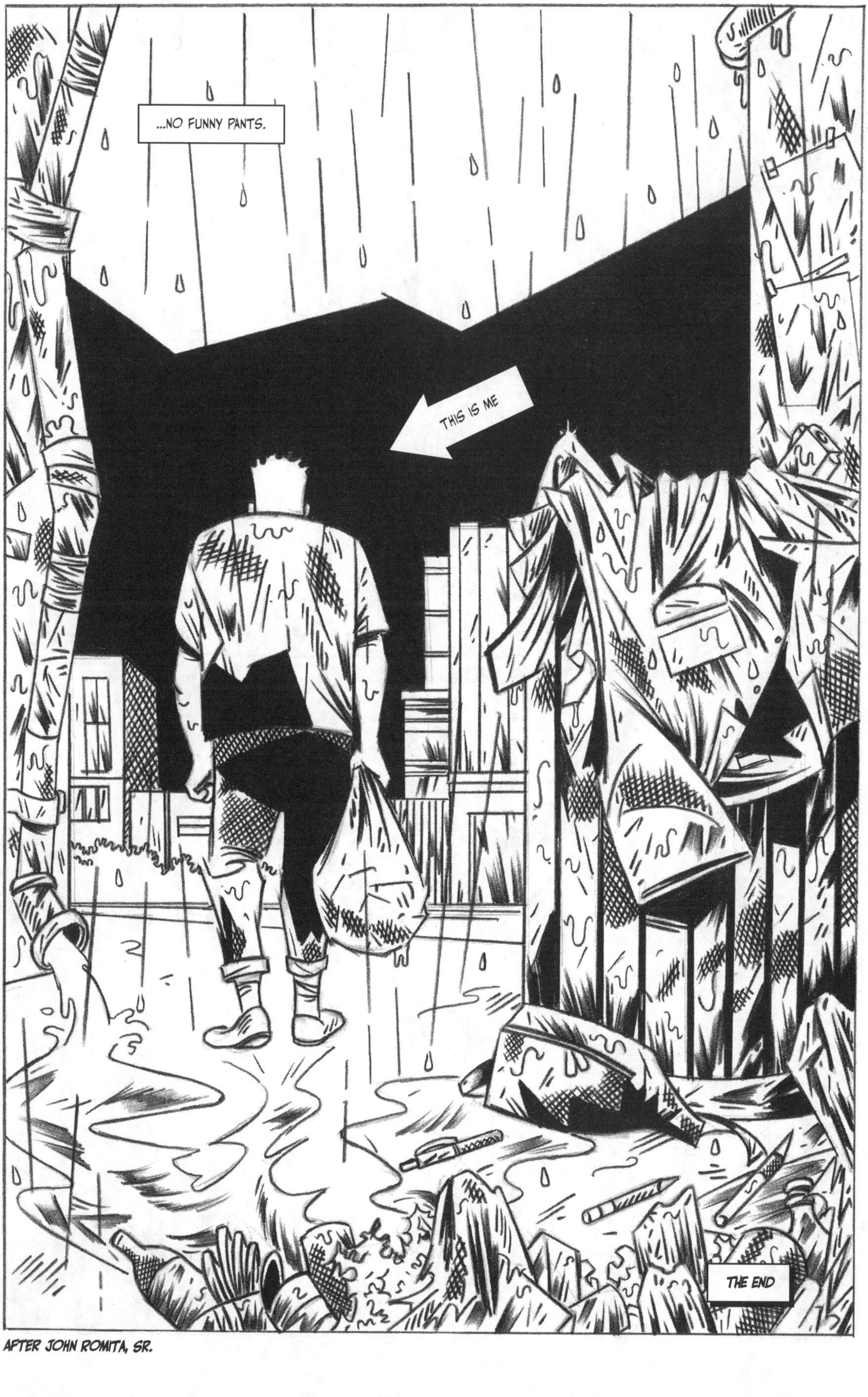
...NO FUNNY PANTS.
THIS IS ME
THE END

AFTER JOHN ROMITA, SR.

ADAM BEECHEN

HENCH

MANNY BELLO

BEHIND THE SCENES

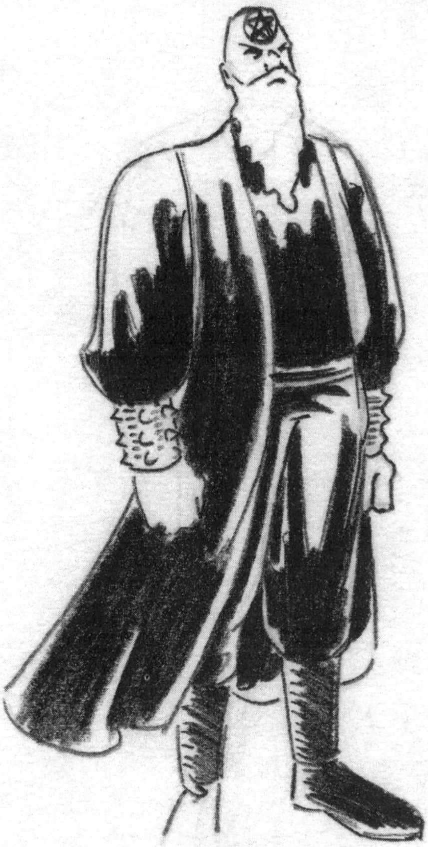

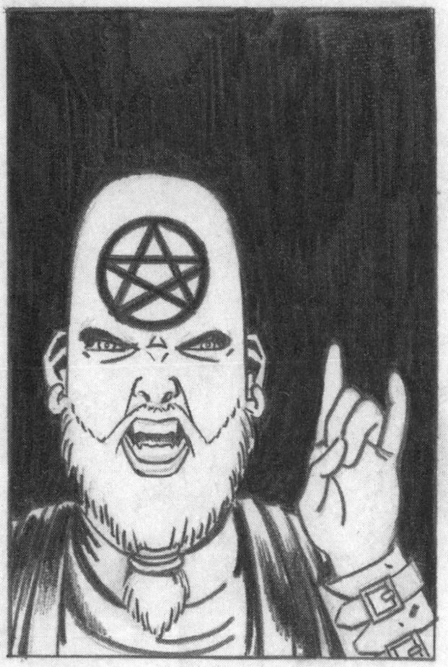

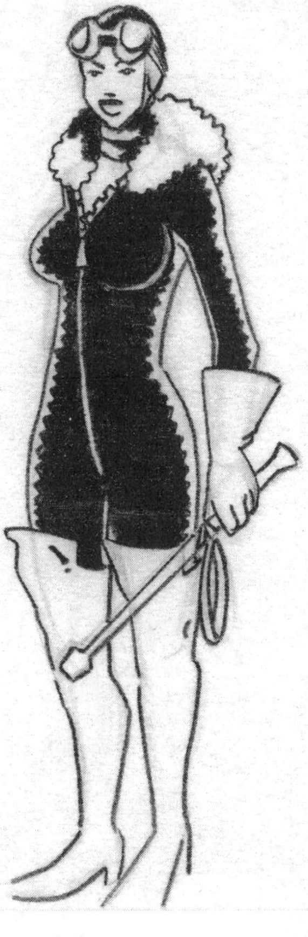

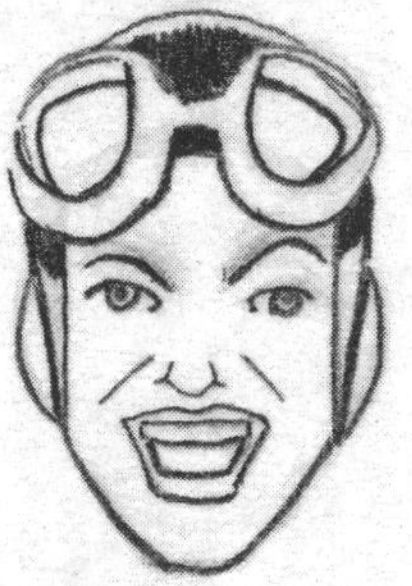

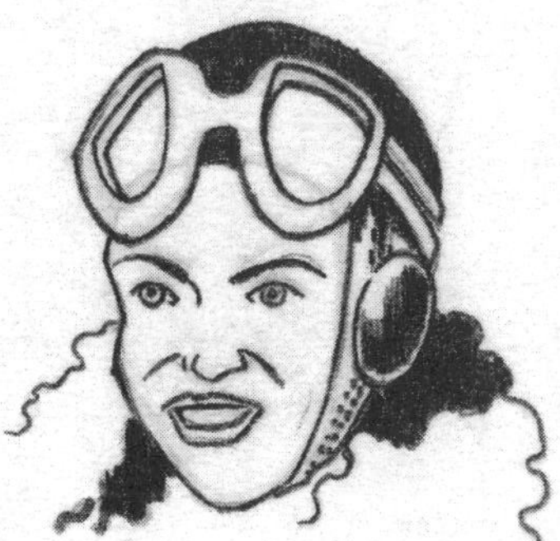

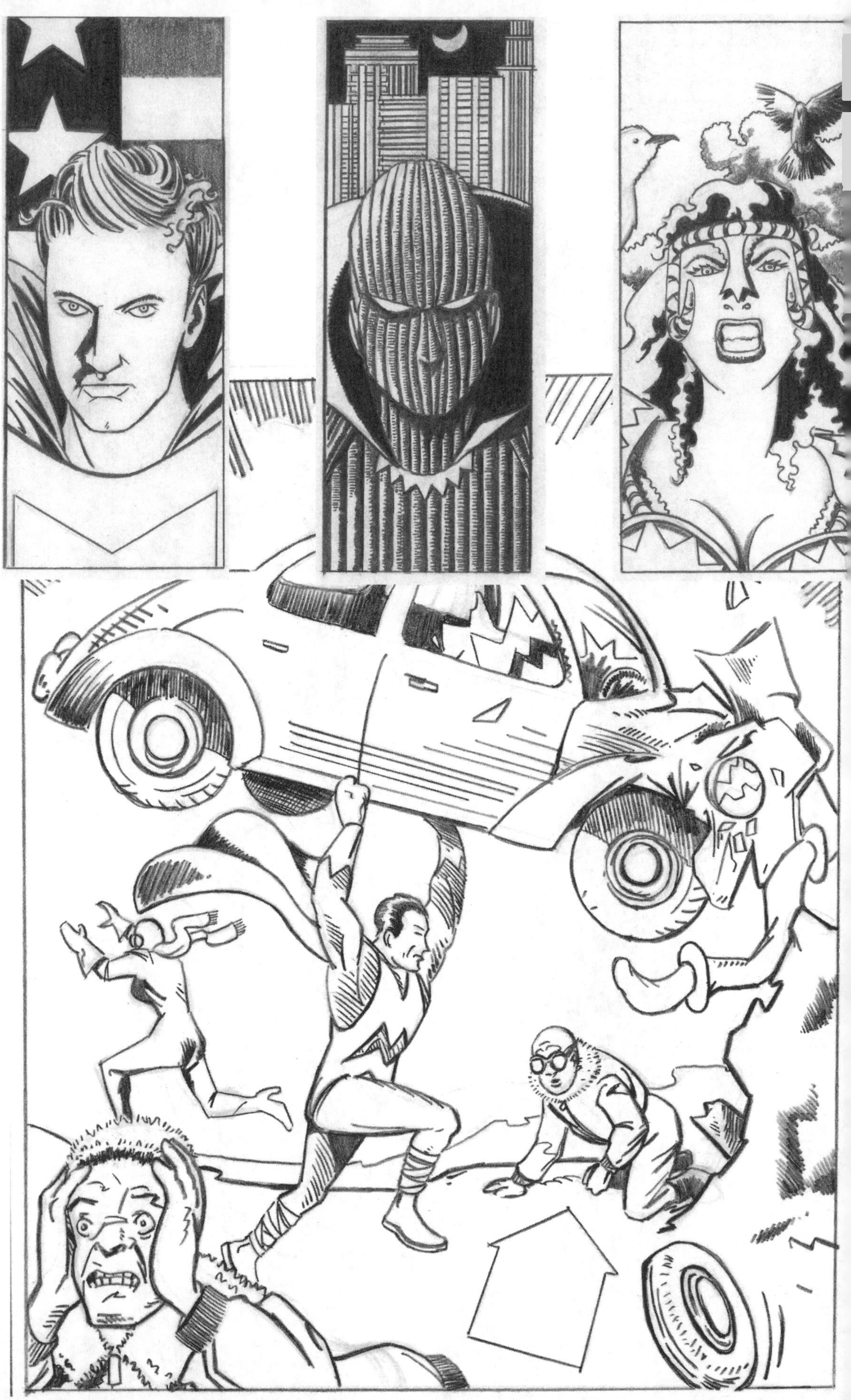

ADAM BEECHEN

HENCH

MANNY BELLO

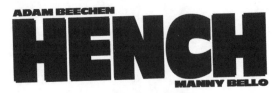

UNUSED PAGES

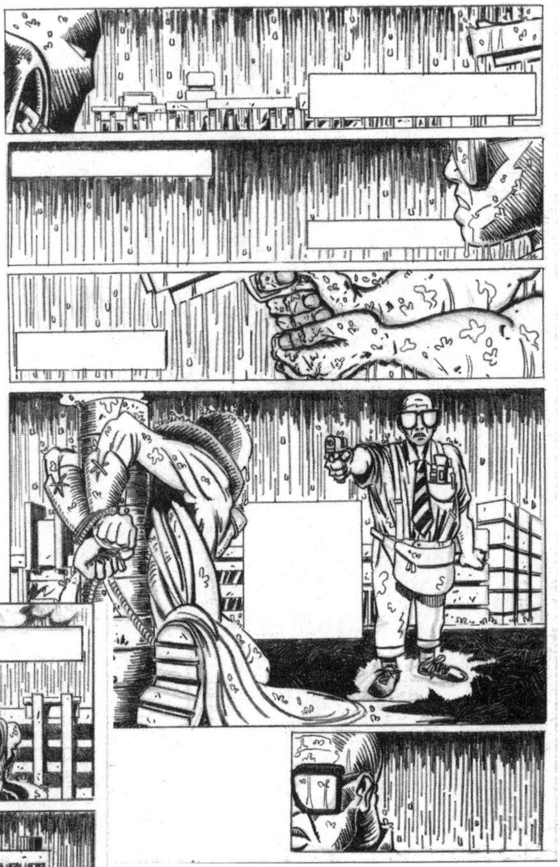

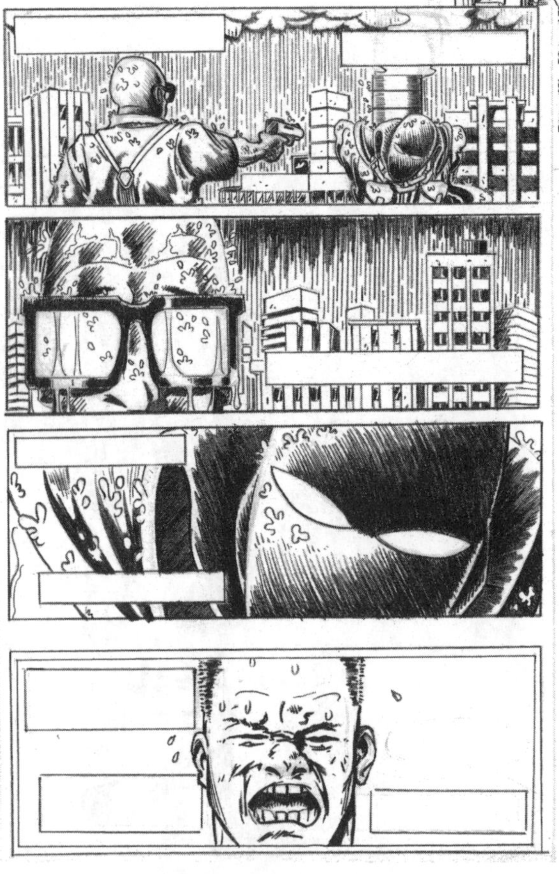

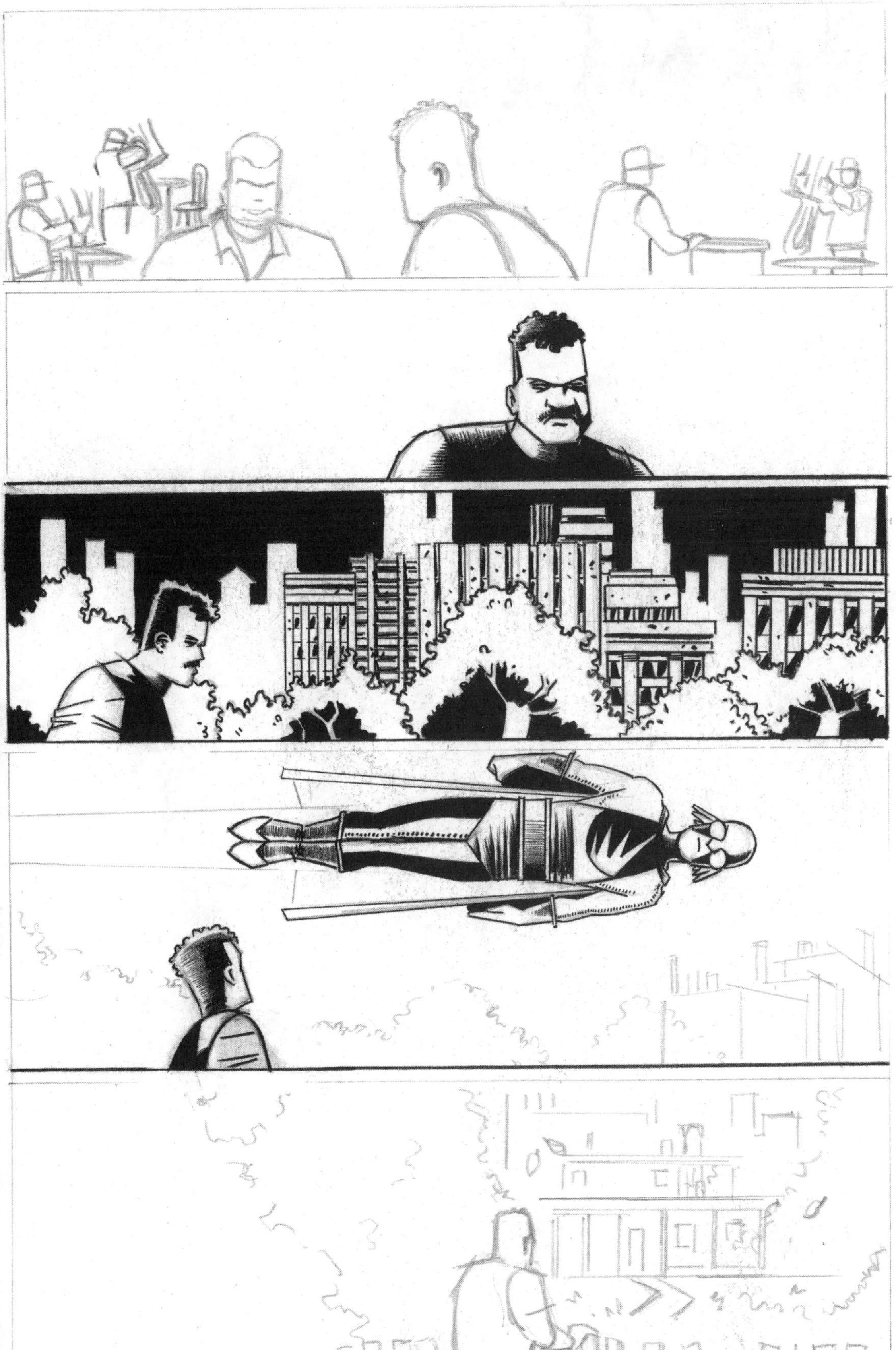

ADAM BEECHEN

HENCH

MANNY BELLO

COVER ROUGHS

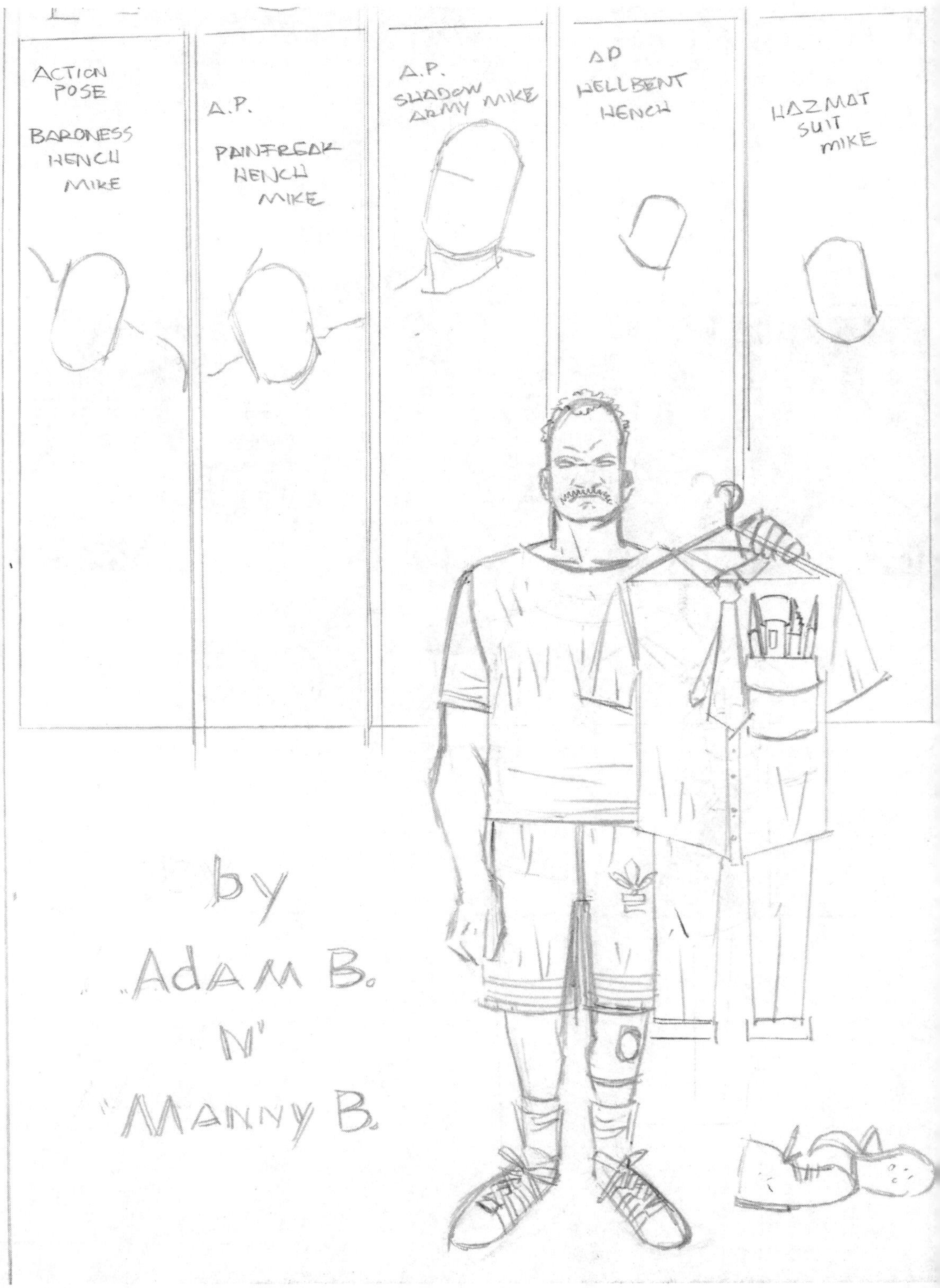

ACTION POSE
BARONESS HENCH MIKE
A.P.
PAINFREAK HENCH MIKE
A.P.
SHADOW ARMY MIKE
AP
HELLBENT HENCH
HAZMAT SUIT MIKE
by
Adam B.
N'
Manny B.

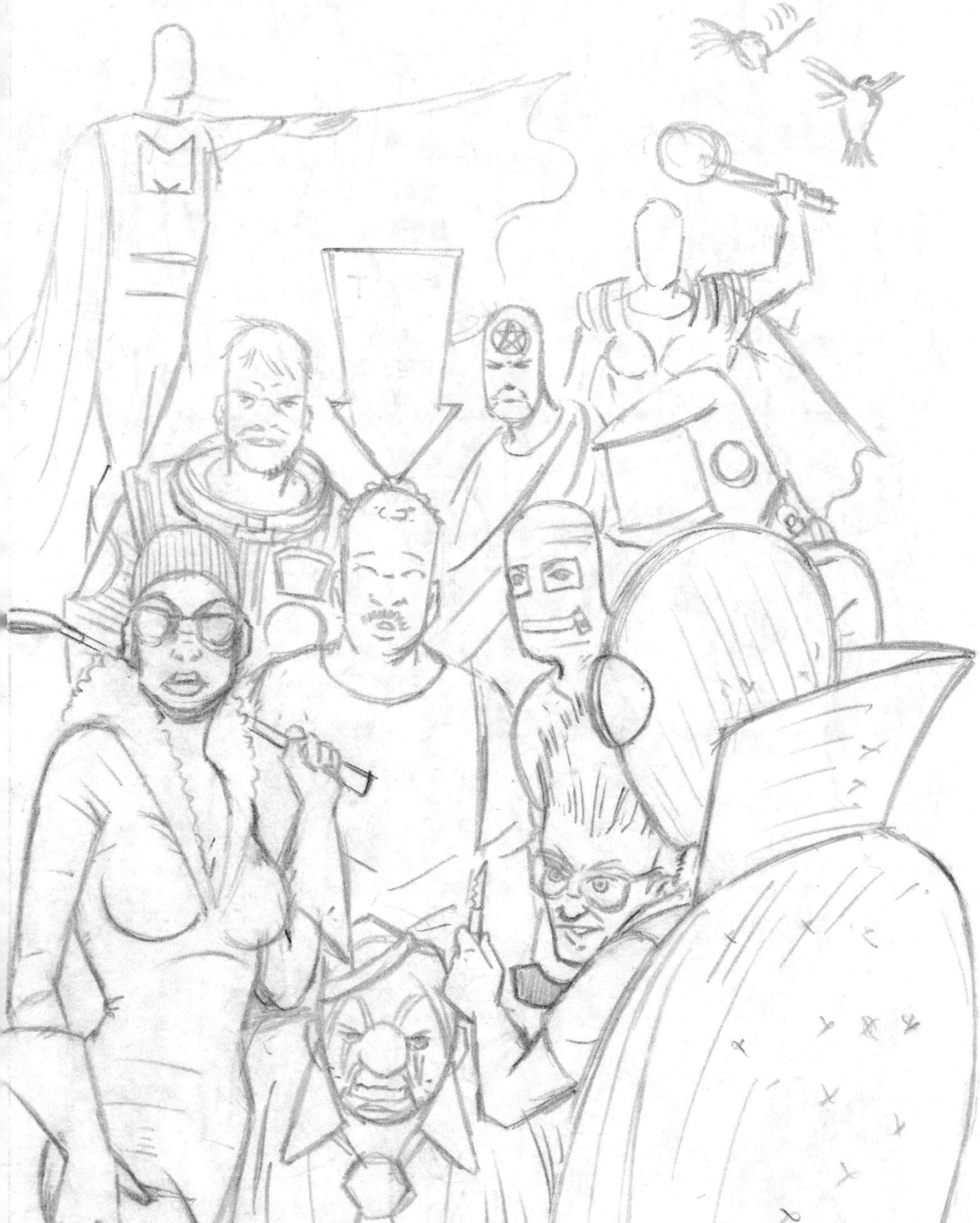

HERE'S MANNY'S COMPLETE COVER ART FOR THE GRAPHIC NOVEL, WITHOUT THE TYPE AND TRADE DRESS.

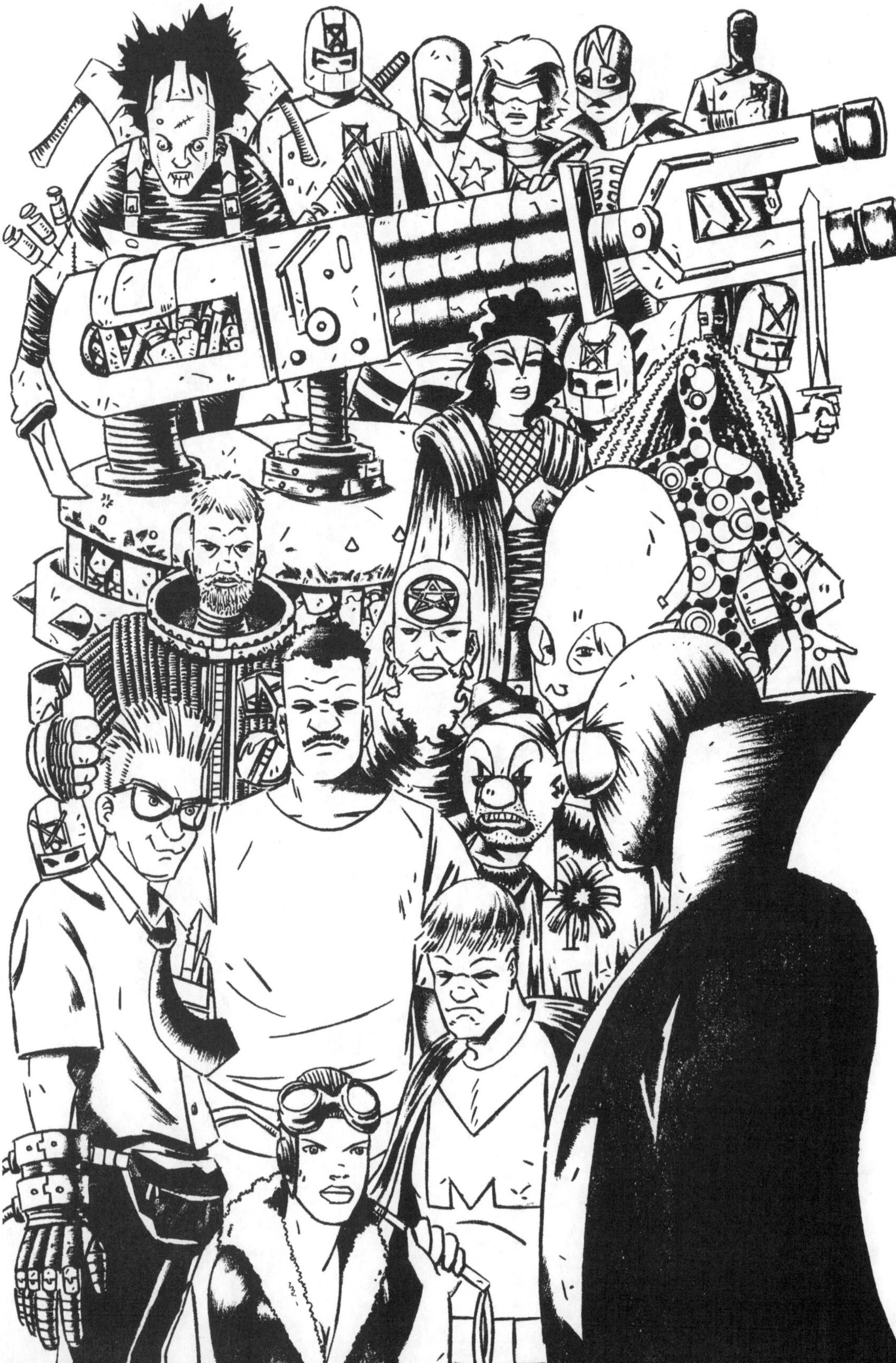